Endorsements

Many years ago I realised that the imagination is a gift from God as much as is the intellect. Revd Dr Peter Stevenson has grasped this with full vigour in this book. The book will take you out of your comfort zones, it will disturb your theology and it will challenge your reading of the Gospels, but most of all it will help you to know and realise that Jesus' actions two millennia ago can bring healing today, to you, to your community, to your nation and to our world.

Revd Dr Jason M E Askew
United Reformed Church Minister and Theologian

Peter Stevenson's new book is a blend of scholarship, imaginative reflection and grounded engagement, revealing that the author is in fact a careful thinker, a preacher and a pastor. This book is a most accessible work that offers both touches of academia and imagination in equal measure, allowing the late modern reader to engage with scripture in a way that opens new doors. I came away from the book wishing I had written it and realising that I have been given a tool that has already revived my inner spiritual child and that is likely to unlock many new ideas from the Gospels.

Revd Dr Howard Worsley
Anglican Priest, Author and Senior Lecturer in Christian Education

Peter Stevenson offers a new take on some well worn (and perhaps therefore overly familiar) healing stories from the gospels. At times quirky and idiosyncratic, often humorous, but always insightful, Stevenson manages to pull off the feat of offering fresh takes on the biblical narratives in question. He does this in a way that is thoroughly congruent for him, by drawing on recent approaches from reader response theory, combined with aspects drawn from his own rhetorical and preaching style to offer an access point to these passages that is startlingly fresh and original. You may not agree with everything that Peter Stevenson says here, but you will be moved to think again about the texts in question and that is surely helpful.

Peter McEnhill
Formerly Director of Studies in Theology at Westminster College, Cambridge

The Healing Beyond the Miracle

Peter Stevenson

Every blessing

P Stevenson

Onwards and Upwards Publishers

Berkeley House, 11 Nightingale Crescent, Leatherhead,
Surrey, KT24 6PD.
www.onwardsandupwards.org

Printed in the UK.

ISBN:	978-1-907509-64-3
Typeface:	Sabon LT
Graphic design:	Leah-Maarit

About the Author

Peter Stevenson was ordained in 2000, moving to London in 2009 as a special category minister within the United Reformed Church encouraged to build a new church, a congregation and a community in the Elephant and Castle. He is married with two children who have both graduated. Peter was educated in Cambridge (Fitzwilliam 2000) and Princeton USA (2009) and holds both a Bachelor of Theology and a Doctor of Ministry.

Peter regularly broadcasts on BBC Radio London. He currently serves Southwark Council (Tooley Street) and Globe Academy as chaplain and is Vice Chair of the Walworth Society.

His hobbies are watching live sport at Wimbledon, Sandown Park, the Oval or Highbury and he loves a night out of fine dining and good conversation with his wife Dawn. Failing that, a night at their local pub is time well spent.

To Revd. Dr Peter McEnhill who
believed in me

To friends and colleagues who
encouraged me

To Dawn and the family who
always support me

Contents

"You did not choose me but I chose you. And I appointed you to go and bear fruit, fruit that will last, so that the Father will give you whatever you ask him in my name."

John 15:16

Preface

During the Spring 2008 Synod of West Midlands United Reformed Church, my colleague Revd. Peter McIntosh was asked to lead the assembly in another way of accessing the meaning of scripture, drawing on his experiences at Crowhurst Christian Healing Centre near Battle, Sussex. He chose to consider Jesus' healing miracles and asked the gathering to suggest an example that came to mind.

What followed was a fascinating interactive sermon highlighting what people knew about the stories, what they thought they knew about them, and what was actually recorded in the text. The exciting aspect of this study was the animated ways in which people began to experience the stories with new insights. The understanding previously overlooked became revelatory. Later analysis of the event made me wonder what was different, and I concluded that the people had been given permission to bring their understandings and misunderstanding to the text without fear of 'mistake'. As a consequence their views were important and added to everyone's overall understanding of how the text worked, what it meant then, and what it means now.

I am grateful to the United Reformed Church for allowing me a sabbatical in 2011 to reflect further and consider how the accounts of Jesus' healing ministry can be used for our benefit in the present age. I am also grateful to Revd. Peter McIntosh for agreeing to supervise my sabbatical and to offer encouragement and comment along the way.

Introduction

"The test of healing is whether it brings the person closer to God, not whether the healing makes them well."

But what of those who attend the person seeking the healing? How does the miracle of healing affect them? Around each person who needs healing are many others who hope and pray for the cure. In what respect does healing heal the friends, neighbours and observers of the one being healed?

"It was a load off my mind when Johnny/Jackie successfully got through his/her cancer scare."

This book seeks to investigate and reflect upon the *healing beyond the miracle* as seen in the examples of Jesus and the effect upon those who witnessed the event. What was the reaction of the four attendants whose friend was healed after they lowered him through the roof of a house where Jesus was speaking? Members of the Temple authorities also witnessed this miracle and we can glimpse their reaction, but what of the others who congregated to listen and learn from Jesus? There are a number of detailed accounts of Jesus' healing miracles and all illustrate different aspects of Christ's healing and the opposition that accompanied them.

Jesus used different methods in his healing ministry. They included: calling upon the faith of the person or bystanders to be healed; touching the sick person; praying; assuring forgiveness of sin; uttering commands and using physical touch. The best-educated people in biblical times had a meagre understanding of human anatomy and physiology and even less knowledge about the nature of disease and its effect on the body. Illness was often attributed to sin or to a curse from an enemy. The main diagnostic tools were observation and superficial physical examination. The New Testament mentions physicians only a few times. Jesus noted the purpose of a physician is to treat the ill (Matt 9:12; Mark 2:17; Luke 5:13) and he referred to a common proverb, "Physician, heal thyself"

(Luke 4:23). Mark and Luke related the story of a woman who had sought the help of physicians but had not been healed (Mark 5:25-34; Luke 8:43-48). Paul, in Colossians 4:14, remarks that his colleague, Luke, was a physician. Luke was a Gentile but his hometown is unknown. The source of his medical training is also unknown, however it is possible that he went to medical school in Tarsus, Paul's hometown. Most of the medicine practiced in ancient Palestine and other outlying parts of the Roman Empire was probably not dispensed by professional physicians and clinicians.

The Bible contains little information about the treatment of disease except through miraculous means. One of Jesus' major ministries was of course healing sick people. They flocked to him in large numbers after having tried all the remedies available in their day. They were often desperate for help and, one imagines, so were their friends, relatives and neighbours. Jesus did not believe that all illness was the direct result of sin (John 9:1-3). He had the power, however, to forgive sin and heal (Matthew 9:1-8; cf. Mark 2:1-12, Luke 5:17-26). Regardless of the cause of their distress, people found that Jesus could truly help.

Accounts of how Jesus cured the sick concentrate on those who received direct healing. I want to investigate and reflect on the effect of that healing on those who attended the sick and witnessed the miracle. Can their example illustrate a healing that takes place after the miracle, and does it have any impact on our lives today?

The obvious problem is going to be how to obtain evidence for *the healing beyond the miracle* without a direct reference to it in the text and without the use of supporting literature from the time. I will employ reader-response criticism and develop creative writing techniques in order to suggest the effect of Jesus' healing miracles on the onlookers and witnesses to the event. For some this may be a new way of looking at scripture; in the prologue I shall survey some other methods of biblical criticism and suggest reasons for using a reader-response approach in this book. The purpose of this approach is to encourage the modern reader to witness the miracles' cumulative effect then and realize how they may be enjoyed now.

This book is for those wanting to take a fresh look at an aspect of Jesus' ministry and consider how healings beyond the miracle can encourage our journey of faith in this age.

Prologue

The Bible is like no other book and must be read in awe and wonder in accordance with its own uniqueness and special rules of discernment. God has spoken plainly through the scribes, the prophets and the interpreters by the power of the Holy Spirit for each generation. There is, however, misunderstanding and misdirection so that the truth remains elusive. As we stray from the original author's intended meaning, there is a danger we may indulge in wildly imaginative interpretations. We must be careful and diligent in maintaining a close connection with past church traditions while recognising the meaning for our age.

Over a number of years, teachers, students and believers have been encouraged to view scripture from a literary and historical perspective. This has led to some excellent scholarship and provided us with tomes exposing wisdom and learning from the great universities of the world. Great insights have been shared, and we are indebted to the careful and painstaking research of brilliant minds and the academic labours of biblical interpreters. However, since the task of the interpretation is to understand the writer's meaning, there is a possibility that interpreters can stray from the writer's true meaning and consequently miss the author's intention.

I am proposing the need to re-employ a degree of imagination – to view the healing miracles of Jesus as stories from which deeper meaning can be extracted than the healings alone. The miracles are described in John's Gospel as signs – parables that illustrate something further. They point to Christ's deity, but they also indicate the Lord's intentions as he uses words like 'faith' and 'saved' in exercising his healing ministry. Physical cure is always associated with spiritual healing, which is why the study of the miracles continues to be a goldmine worthy of our quarrying today. Miracles can teach us how Christ saves lives and on what terms.

John 20:30-31

Now Jesus did many other signs in the presence of his disciples, which are not written in this book. But these are written so that you may come to believe that Jesus is the Messiah, the Son of God and that through believing you may have life in his name.

We must, of course, pay the closest attention to the literal meaning of Jesus' healing miracles in their historical context, but we should not limit or exhaust our work of interpretation because the Bible is like no other book. Paul writes:

Romans 15:4

For whatever was written in former days was written for our instruction, so that by steadfastness and by the encouragement of the scriptures we might have hope.

It should be part of our journey of faith to engage and wrestle with the text so that we might be helped to realize the fullness of blessing that the Lord wishes for all.

If the starting point is the biblical text and the goal is to understand the healing miracles of Jesus in context, what device can be use to span the divide? Interpreting the Bible is often described in terms of various criticisms: historical, literary, source, form, redaction and textual (see below). However, these have become the preserve of the trained professional and the average reader has increasingly been asked to accept this interpretation rather than encouraged to find their own path of understanding. This book offers a different opportunity; we will view the text from the perspective of reader-response criticism, in which the reader inhabits the story, discovers the meaning for themselves and identifies how their interpretation applies to their own context. This technique is explored in greater detail below.

Historical Criticism

This criticism comes from nineteenth century European universities, especially Halle-Wittenberg, through the studies and writings of Friedrich Daniel Ernst Schleiermacher (1768 - 1834), who was influenced by Johann Salomo Semler (1725 - 1791). This approach seeks to find the particular historical setting or settings of the writings. Dating the text becomes crucial, and external resources such as archaeological evidence or non-biblical writings from the same period are greatly prized. Setting the writing in its historical context enables interpreters to expound the meaning and purpose of the text leading, in preaching terms, to an explanation for the present context.

Literary Criticism

This approach is concerned with the structures, themes and language of the text. It identifies types of genre being employed, such as narrative, poetic, apocalyptic, oratorical, and rhetorical, and analyzes the grammar and language of the original text. By evaluating the words used and their various meanings, or shades of meanings, supporters of this interpretative style believe that it is possible to discover the writer's meaning and therefore arrive at the truths contained. This approach is not only employed in a religious context but also widely used in more general writings.

Source Criticism

Source Criticism begins with the hypothesis that the biblical writings as we now have them are a combination of once distinct written documents that were only later brought together. A good example of how this approach was employed can be seen in the work of Julius Wellhausen (1844 - 1918) who developed a theory for the divisions in the first five books of the Hebrew Bible. An earlier division between Yahwistic and Elohimic sources had been suggested to explain the different titles of God used. Wellhausen proposed two additional sources were evident and described them as Priestly and Deuteronomic. His argument is that these sources have their own unique historical and literary foundations and by separating them into their sources the text can be understood with greater clarity.

Form Criticism

This approach is another hybrid of historical and literary criticisms and is concerned with discerning the story, legend and myth that lies behind the text. It begins with the recognition that a portion of a text may have a history of its own, independent of the larger work in which it is located. Hermann Gunkel (1862 - 1932) and his nephew Sigmund Mowinkel (1884 - 1965) are notable supporters of this approach and studied the instances where the same biblical text occurs in different parts of the Bible in different forms. By studying these instances they sought meaning and understanding for the context then and now.

Redaction Criticism

The major emphasis of this approach is concerned with when and by what process of collecting and editing did a particular section or book of the Bible reach its final literary form. The text is analyzed for individual instances where the editor has redacted an earlier text. This is then assessed for the overall significance of the change and interpreted in light of the literary and theological purpose. The original use of this method of criticism was restricted to the synoptic Gospels of Matthew, Mark and Luke.

Textual Criticism

This is sometimes called lower criticism, not because it is considered inferior or less important but because it deals with the actual wording of scripture. It is concerned with ancient manuscripts and what an author actually wrote. Such a method is unlikely to achieve its goals as the original manuscripts almost certainly do not exist and the various surviving copies do not always agree and are often incomplete. In addition, there are thousands of manuscripts dating from the third to the sixteenth centuries to be considered. 'Best guess assessment' is possible when all these factors are taken into account. The Nestle-Aland, Novum Testamentum Graece offers helpful insights into the various codices, parchments and fragments that have been used to formulate the Christian Bible as we know it.

The Difficulties with These Approaches to Biblical Interpretation

In one sense there are no difficulties in these approaches as they have served the church well and have enabled scholars to understand different elements and nuances of the text. Modern scholarship continues to help people gain insight into almost every aspect of the text, going deeper into the textual, historic or literary significance of various passages. But the benefit of this is also its cost. The people for whom the book is meant often feel inhibited from studying the primary text and have largely lost control of the meaning, to the extent that many wait for the interpretation of others rather than wrestle with the text themselves. This is not the fault of the scholar who is merely following academic requirements and expectation, but the faithful follower feels ill equipped to tackle the learning needed by these approaches.

A new opportunity does exist for the faithful to learn from the text directly and allow the guidance of the Holy Spirit to inform, encourage and educate. It simply requires another way of reading and understanding the scriptures. I believe that reader-response criticism offers this opportunity.

Reader-Response Criticism

If a piece of writing were to start, "Once upon a time..." the reader would be expecting a fairy tale to follow and would approach the writing on that basis. They would put reality to one side and suspend belief in order to understand the tale being told. Similarly if a text were to begin, "It was a dark and stormy night..." the reader might reasonably expect a horror or ghost story. A love story might begin with the embrace of two people looking lovingly into the other's eyes. An opening such as, "The bald camel walking along Elephant and Castle High Street was suddenly stopped in its tracks by an axe-wielding aardvark," would make the reader wonder what was coming next, and unless they were accustomed to the author's style they would need to read on to establish the genre being encountered.

What then might be the response to an opening phrase, "In the beginning was the Word and the Word was with God and the Word was God."? It is impossible for a reader to be neutral when they approach text without bringing understanding, experience and expectation. There is a story (the text), a storyteller (the narrator) and a story reader (the interpreter). It is the interaction between these three that reader-response criticism seeks to establish. Naturally the narrator is able to see the whole of the road – unlike the interpreter, who can see only what lies immediately before them.

Wolfgang Iser helpfully plots the development in patterns of communication chronologically from Bunyan to Beckett. He refers to Pilgrim's Progress as "a book meant to appeal to each individual reader, whatever his disposition and its aim is to lead the believer to recognize himself." [1] As the epic gives way to the novel, the relationship between story, narrator and interpreter changes.

The author creates, in short, an image of himself and another image of his reader; he makes his reader, as he makes his second self and the most successful reading is one in which the created selves, author and reader, can find complete agreement. [2]

The reader is not alone in the task of interpretation as there is a collective consciousness that regulates our approach to the text and helps us to avoid nonsense interpretations. The role of the reader in terms of the narrator is something potential and not actual; the narrator cannot guarantee the reader's response and can only hope that the story conveys the narrator's intention accurately to a receptive reader. There is therefore scope for a great number of individual pictures to formulate. Literary criticism has been mainly concerned with the author's point of view, paying little attention to how the reader might be affected. The reader is not merely a spectator and their response is crucial to understanding the story and the narrator's intention. Establishing the author-reader relationship is key to understanding the story.

As the reader uses the various perspectives offered to him by the text in order to relate the patterns and the schematized views to one another, he sets the work in motion and this very process results ultimately in the awakening of responses within himself. [3]

It is in the process of bringing imagination to the text that the story comes alive; without the need for imagination to enter the field, the result would be boredom. I wonder if this is the reason why so many say that they cannot read the Bible? Is it also why so much reliance is placed on the professional who can explain the meaning of a text? By introducing another influence to the three-way relationship of story, storyteller and reader – that of interlocutor – is there a

---

[1] Wolfgang Iser, *The Implied Reader: Pattern of Communication in Prose Fiction from Bunyan to Beckett* (London, The John Hopkins University Press, 1974), p7.

[2] Wayne C. Booth, *The Rhetoric of Fiction* (Chicago, 1963), p138 cited in Implied Reader p 30

[3] Ibid., p275

danger that we lose one of them? The Bible has an episode supporting the use of an interlocutor in the story of Philip and the Ethiopian eunuch reading from the book of Isaiah on his way back to Queen Candace's treasury (Acts 8:26-40). Philip as interlocutor was vital to the reader's understanding of a story that made no sense. However, it is the writer who introduces the interlocutor for the purpose of understanding, and so the reader of this story is to recognize the interlocutor as part of the story rather than independent of it. The story would be an interesting study in reader-response criticism but falls outside the scope of this book. What it does highlight is the way the story can be used to interpret the message that the writer intends for the reader and how multifarious the text becomes.

The writer brings the words and the reader brings the meaning, but is the writer content with the meaning that the reader brings? Does the story convey the meaning that the writer intends, and is it necessary for such meaning to be understood only by the reader the writer has in mind when telling the story? Understanding the reader is essential to reader-response criticism. Theorists divide into three groups: individualists, experimenters and uniformists. The individualists believe the reader controls the meaning while the experimenters and uniformists put the text in control. However, all approaches continue to seek the relationship between story, teller and reader. Wolfgang Iser exemplifies the latter theorists' approach. For him, a literary work is not an object in itself but an effect to be explained and he asserts that this response is controlled by the text. The reader's activities are confined within limits set by the literary work. He suggests that "an ideal reader would have an identical code to that of the author." [4] It could be argued therefore that the ideal reader is the writer but then the story becomes locked in the writer's own intention. What this book tries to do is allow the reader to break free of the shackles that prevent the reader from the interpretative experience of the stories. Reader-response criticism allows the reader to take charge, allowing them to use their experience, knowledge and understanding in order to draw meaning from the text.

Although the story may incorporate the social norms and values of its time, its function is not merely to present such data but to use

---

[4] Wolfgang Iser. *The Act of Reading: A Theory of Aesthetic Response.* (London: The John Hopkins University Press, 1978), p28.

them in order to direct the reader into the story and its meaning for them. Text will come alive when the reader becomes productive and seeks the meaning and interpretation of the story. The writer's task is to encourage the reader to engage with the story and make it personal with meaning and value for them. Tompkins suggests that "reader and writer join hands, change places and finally become distinguished only as two names for the same activity." [5] The book is an object full of potential that cannot be realized while it remains on the shelf. The story can only live in the hands of the reader. The writer, having done the work of storytelling, can play no further part but wait until the reader brings the words to life.

So who is the reader in reader-response criticism and who would the writer want to read the story? Is it you – the reader of this book? Surveying the literature of these studies and the theorist's description provides a list of possibilities below with brief explanations.

- *The Real Reader*
  A person who is physically holding the book.

- *The Critical Reader*
  Expert readers able to critique the work from a number of academic viewpoints.

- *The Ideal Reader*
  A person able to read and interpret works in ways which others find acceptable

- *The Implied Reader*
  The writer creates an image of themselves and an image of the reader. The most successful reading of the story occurs when there is complete agreement between the two. (See above)

- *The Hypothetical Reader*
  A reasonable, fair-minded person of ordinary intelligence with a degree of general knowledge able to understand the text but without interpretative skills necessarily.

---

[5] Jane P. Tompkins. *Reader-Response Criticism: From Formalism to Post-Structuralism.* (London: The John Hopkins University Press Ltd., 1980), p.x

- *The Contemporary Reader*
  A person who understands the writing in terms of their own culture and context

- *The Post-Modern Reader*
  Similar to the contemporary reader, but understanding the writing in terms of a set of criteria that supports the view that the present culture and context is informed by modernity.

- *The Intended Reader*
  A reader whose education, opinion, concerns and linguistic competences make them capable of having the understanding and experience the writer wished to provide.

- *The Super Reader*
  A person who is an informed and competent critic.

- *The Informed Reader*
  Similar to the Super reader, they are able to read with knowledge of the context and culture of the writer, but may not necessarily be able to interpret for the present age.

Each type, or description, of reader will be of use and help in reading different genres of story (text). Reading sacred writings will benefit from some more than another. Reader-response criticism with respect to the Gospels is not so much concerned with what the text says or shows but with what the text does to the reader. After all, "readers are not passive receivers of data but active participants in the production of meaning and the creation of significance." [6]

Two books that explore how to use the Christian Bible in modern context have been published. Jerry Camery-Hoggatt's title, *Reading the Good Book Well,* [7] is a guide to biblical interpretation employing textual, literary and historic criticisms, while Robert M. Fowler looks at reader-response criticism in the Gospel of Mark in his work

---

[6] Sandra Hack Polaski, *Identifying the Unnamed Disciple: An Exercise in Reader-Response Criticism,* Perspectives in Religious Studies 26 (1999), 193-202. accessed 040110 via ATLAS

[7] Jerry Camery-Hoggatt. *Reading the Good Book Well: A Guide to Biblical Interpretation.* (Nashville, TN, USA: Abingdon Press, 2007).

entitled *Let the Reader Understand.* [8] Both are recommended for their thorough biblical and scholarly content and come with academic endorsements and supporters. They are not opposing views as both seek to understand the gospel story but from different perspectives.

Naturally this book leans heavier on the work of Fowler than Camery-Hoggatt in trying to get its interpreter to view criticism of the sacred text from a reader-response viewpoint. The former criticisms are not outdated, ineffective or without value, but there is a need for the scriptures to be viewed by the faithful in personal and refreshing ways. As Camery-Hoggatt says, "It isn't enough to ask what the Bible says. We also have to ask what it means." [9] As Paul says in his letter to Timothy:

> **2 Timothy 3:16-17**
> *All scripture is inspired by God and profitable for teaching, for reproof, for correction and for training in righteousness, that the man of God may be complete, equipped for every good work.*

The concern for Camery-Hoggett is that the potential for individualism in reader-response criticism allows for any interpretation. In clear terms he says, "The inescapable, non-negotiable, take-it-to-the-bank point is that we're not free to draw whatever conclusions we want just because they may make sense to us." [10] He characterizes language as:

- *Selective*
  It can't say everything, but has to omit some things

- *Inherently ambiguous*
  Words can sometimes carry double (or multiple) meanings.

- *Polyvalent*
  Carrying meaning on different levels – emotional, cognitive, social and personal

---

[8] Robert M. Fowler. *Let the Reader Understand: Reader-Response Criticism and the Gospel of Mark.* (Harrisburg, Pennsylvania, USA: Trinity Press International paperback edition, 2001).
[9] Reading the Good Book Well p5
[10] Ibid., p72

- *Linear*
  It can only present its information in a specific sequence, one word after another [11]

He argues that the reader is "not free to fill in gaps however we please; we have to do that in a way that's consistent with what the author expected the authorial reader to do." [12] I agree that the process of interpretation is the way that the gaps are filled. The preferred way for Camery-Hoggatt draws heavily on previous criticisms, but even he recognizes that getting the right system is crucial if the reader is not to miss what the Bible is actually saying. It is right that he encourages the reader to understand the social and cultural norms of first century society; to have an understanding of the linguistics, language and lexicography of biblical text; and to know the historical setting and progression of God's people. However, none of these will necessarily provide application to an individual's own context and they do not address how God, through the Holy Spirit, by the power of Jesus, uses the text to speak to a person today.

Fowler recommends:

> ...a shift away from looking for a static structure in the text toward an awareness of the dynamic, temporal experience of reading the text ... Once [the] experience is the focus of criticism, the meaning of meaning also needs to be reinterpreted. No longer can meaning be understood to be stable, determinate content that lies buried within the text, awaiting excavation. Rather, meaning becomes a dynamic event in which we ourselves participate. Furthermore, the shift from meaning-as-content to meaning-as-event leads us to understand the workings of the language of the Gospel in new ways. No longer can the language of the Gospel be regarded as primarily referential or informative. It has become rhetorical, affective and powerful. [13]

The reader in reader-response criticism is not simply the reader. Anyone can read the text without comment or interpretation; an example of this could be the holiday reader of fiction wanting simply to be transported into another world of the author's making without

---

[11] Ibid., p76
[12] Ibid., p78
[13] *Let the Reader Understand* p3

being concerned about meaning or consideration. There must be a degree of critique if there is to be interpretative value. Quoting Steiner, Fowler says, "...the critic is judge and master of the text, whereas the reader is servant to the text." [14] There needs to be objectivity and deliberate critical engagement with the text if the reader-response approach is not simply a comment about "what the passage means to me." Stanley Fish talks about the need for the 'interpretive community'; this is a useful corrective to those who dislike the approach of reader-response criticism because of what they perceive as an individualistic exercise preventing absolute truth being collectively ascribed. I subscribe to Fowler's view that reader-response criticism should focus on the reader; the reader frequently fixes their own meaning to the text at the moment of reading.

James Resseguie takes us on one last excursion before we begin to look at the healing miracles of Jesus from a reader-response perspective. He uses a narrative critical approach to discover the author's intended story. "Like a complex and intriguing puzzle," he offers, "narrative analysis enlivens the imagination and offers new ways of looking at the familiar." [15] He offers the bridge between classical criticisms and reader-response, paying close attention to the narrative as a whole and looking for its nuances. He examines New Testament literature not as history or dogma, or as social or political criticism, but by understanding the literariness of the text and its literary qualities. He uses devises such as plot, setting, characterisation, rhetoric and point of view in order to help understand the Gospels. This would be similar to the literary approach above, except he adds the reader into the process and asks:

1. What expectations are developed in the (implied) reader and how are they fulfilled or frustrated as the narrative proceeds?
2. What new, defamilarised point of view results from the fulfilling or overturning of expectations?
3. What is the new point of view the narrator wants the reader to adopt? How is the reader to view reality differently? [16]

---

[14] Ibid., p27, quoting George Steiner. *Critic/Reader* NLH (1979): 423-52
[15] James L. Resseguie. *Narrative Criticism of the New Testament: An Introduction.* (Grand Rapids, MI, USA: Baker Academic, 2005). p241.
[16] Ibid., p244

It can be seen that the focus is on the writer; only in relationship to the writer does the reader have an interpretative function. The approach that this book offers is not reliant on other academic disciplines but assumes a received knowledge of the Christian faith and an eagerness to engage with the text in order to develop meaning and understanding. This way of reading the text critically gives the interpretative function to the reader and does not rely on an interlocutor, a historian or a literary expert.

As we now approach Jesus' healing miracles in the following chapters, we will concentrate on the effect of the miracles to the people who attended. As the title of this book indicates, we will not simply view the miracles from the position of the person who was cured but aim to understand what the healing meant to the friends, family and observers who witnessed it. How did the community change by what they saw, and what was the impact on the society? Can the miracle that happened then make a difference to our thinking now?

CHAPTER ONE

From the Beginning

Let us start with Mark's recording of Jesus' first two healing miracles, that of the exorcism of the unclean spirit which gripped a worshipper in the synagogue and the healing of Peter's mother-in-law in a private house one hundred metres down the road.

The first Markan miracle is also the first public appearance of Jesus following his baptism, when he is invited to preach in the synagogue, a privilege afforded to few. It might be deduced that Jesus had a strong reputation prior to the appearance and meant that he was accepted and recognised in the area. Capernaum was situated on the north west shore of Galilee and was the village where seven other miracles took place: the healing of the paralytic (see Chapter Three); the healing of the man with a withered hand (see Chapter Six); the healing of a blind mute; the healing of Jairus' daughter, which is linked with the healing of the haemorrhaging woman (see Chapter Two); the healing of two blind men (Chapter Four); and the healing of the mute demoniac.

Jesus chose to call his first disciples Simon Andrew, James and John from Capernaum, and Matthew the tax collector was also from the village. Originally from Bethsaida a few miles east, Simon and Andrew had moved to the area in search of the better fishing trade. The village of Kfar Nahum was accepted as a harbour from where good catches could be had.

These two miracles take place during the Sabbath, between sunsets on Friday and Saturday. In all, seven Sabbath healing miracles take place. The other five are the man with a withered hand, the

25

crippled woman, the man with dropsy, the paralytic at Bethesda, and the man born blind. Naturally, much is written about Jesus healing on the Sabbath in opposition and defiance to the temple authorities, which is considered further in Chapter Six. Jesus and the disciples entered the synagogue on Friday evening after the fishermen had finished work earlier in the day. There are many differences between the exorcism and the healing: one is in public, the other in private; one drives out demon unclean spirit(s) that convulse the victim, while the other brings the blessing of cure and results in gratitude; a man in the first and a woman in the second; a stranger with a troubled soul, unlike the friend and extended family member; one responds to Jesus' voice while the other is comforted by his touch.

If you were present in the synagogue, how would you react to the sudden outburst of a man crying out, "Have you come to destroy us?" The onlookers were astounded and amazed by the authority with which Jesus had preached. Like a breath of fresh air Jesus' teachings were unlike those of the scribes who moralized and pushed for a pious, heavily law-bound way of living the faith. Suddenly the worshippers were confronted with a challenge to which Jesus responds, "Be silent and come out of him." It certainly cannot be compared with a well-aimed rebuke from a seasoned orator to a heckling sceptic because what followed was even more dramatic: the accuser was thrown to the floor in a convulsing fit.

Reading back in the text one might reflect whether the man was really ill; we learn that he was not right because of what followed Jesus' rebuke, but how did his illness present itself prior to the incident? Both gospel writers Mark (1:21-18) and Luke (4:33-38) suggest that he appears as an unclean man, but his disease appears to be confined to calling out. There are many occasions walking along the street in London that I pass people who call out for no apparent reason, and I am not sure that I would take fright as a result. The recorded words do not appear to be particularly inflammatory, naming Jesus as from Nazareth and following it with a title "The Holy One of God." So, it is perhaps the manner of how the titles were directed that was notable; it was not *what* was said but *how* it was said.

The man displayed something in his tone or delivery that confirmed a deeper illness, later recorded as the man's demonic possession. The man's "spirit is at odds with the divine ordering, though not necessarily irrevocably evil". [17] As Hooker points out it is strange that he is allowed into the synagogue given his demon possession, but maybe it is only now that it has materialised. This is where the reader can imagine the circumstances and scene as the story unfolds. The result is that Jesus' fame begins to spread throughout the surrounding region of Galilee.

In that case let us consider the *healing beyond the miracle*. If we attend the synagogue in the role of leader, or worshipper, or visitor, *what have we experienced?* As a worshipper we had expected the same old service of prayers, benedictions, readings from the law and the prophets, together with a message delivered by the priests. The leader has allowed a new man to speak, and as he starts we realise something is different; we are already aware and alert to a new thing happening. We sit up and listen with a greater intensity and learn new meanings as a result. Our faith is alive and awakened by this new interpretation, and we are happy for the service to last longer than the usual forty five minutes.

Perhaps at the height of Jesus' teaching there is a commotion resulting from an untimely outburst from one of the regulars who is suddenly calling out and disrupting the service. We are about to jeer and admonish the heckler when he starts writhing on the ground; the visitor takes control of the situation and commands the unclean spirit to go. To our utter amazement all is calm and the moment has passed. We are left to reflect, is he the man we have been waiting for? Is he the Messiah? Did we really see what we think we saw? As we hurry off to tell our family, friends and neighbours, a hope is reawakened deep within us that national pride and self-respect could once again be ours.

We also think this is a good opportunity to get the visitor to help with a loved one who is suffering from ill health, ailments and general malaise and commit ourselves to bringing them to him as soon as Sabbath is over. Ensuring that we know where he is staying, we return to our family.

As we leave this scene behind we travel with the disciples to the next healing found of Peter's mother-in-law on the pages of Mark

---

[17] Hooker, Morna D. *The Gospel According to St Mark.* London: A & C Black (publishers) Ltd., 1991. P64

1:29-31, Matthew 8:14-15 and Luke 4:38-39. Before the reader even opens the books, what is already known about this story?

- Where does it take place?
- When does it happen?
- Who is healed?
- What was the illness?
- Who are the witnesses?
- What was the result?

Mark's account makes the answers to these questions easy to establish. He tells us that the setting is Simon Peter and Andrew's house, on the Sabbath after participation in the synagogue. Simon Peter's mother-in-law is unwell in bed with a fever. The healing occurs in the presence of at least the four named disciples, when Jesus takes the unnamed lady by the hand and lifts her from her bed. As a result she is able to serve *them*.

Matthew however places this story among many other healing accounts and gives the reader less detail or context. He simply says that Jesus enters Peter's house and on seeing Peter' mother-in-law unwell in bed with a fever, Jesus touches the unnamed woman's hand and she gets up to serve *him*.

Luke's account is closer to that of Mark and he agrees the timing and citing of the healing but adds emphasis to the diagnosis, calling it a high fever. The healing is effected without physical contact, and Jesus is reported as "[standing] over her and rebuking the fever." Either way, she was cured and able to serve them. An aside here is that calling Simon Peter and the others to be disciples comes after this miracle in Luke's account.

The common thread is that there was a woman who became well enough to rise from her sickbed in order to provide service as a result of Jesus' healing intervention.

As the reader of the story what do you see? What other questions come to mind?

What was Simon Peter's wife doing? We can assume that she was with Peter from a later reference in Paul's letter (1 Corinthians 9:5), where we learn that Peter's wife accompanied him. So where was she in this story as her mother lay stretched out, prone, suffering in a feverish state? Perhaps the reader would wish to take her place in the story and experience the emotion of having a sick mother and an important guest arriving – possibly unannounced – on the Sabbath, along with a number of other invited/uninvited guests. What is your response to the healing that Jesus performs, and do you encourage Mum to start to work?

The miracle shows us:

- *The importance of intercession.*
  Others become the channel of blessing for someone else.

- *While there are times to relax and get away, ministry sometimes needs to be done when we are tired.*
  Jesus had just been teaching in the synagogue and he has been invited back to Peter's house to eat and rest, but necessity dictated otherwise.

- *Serving should be the natural response of gratitude for the work of God in our lives.*
  The mother-in-law got up and immediately began to wait on them. Luke and Mark both point this out. Luke points it out because as a doctor, he wants to emphasize the completeness of the healing. Mark points it out because it fits his theme of serving.

- *Being a follower of Jesus does not exempt our family from sickness.*

- *Sickness can be used to teach us what to do with our health.*
  There is no better time to reflect on what is important to us when the opportunity to do it is taken away from us.

If this was a typical devout Jewish household the Sabbath meal would have been prepared in the afternoon to avoid working on the holy day. We might reasonably deduce this to be the evening main meal after worship when the family eats leisurely and often talks about God. The disciples were present at the synagogue and have only just accepted Jesus' call on their lives. What would be their thinking as they walked the short distance from the place of worship to the house? As reader you are encouraged to pause and reflect on what you would want to ask Jesus about the future should you choose to follow him and respond to the offer he makes: "Follow me and I will make you fish for people." (Mark 1:17)

Was the incident in the synagogue a foretaste of what the future was going to be like? Would there be astonishment and amazement wherever they went? What would be their role – bodyguard, crowd control, acolyte? You, the reader will have your own questions to pose, but we will all have to wait as we enter the house to learn of illness and (high) fever gripping our matriarch. Incidentally, there is only one other story about a mother-in-law in scripture; it tells of the relationship between Ruth and Naomi, and that resulted in the line of David being established.

The result of this healing does not quite have the same impact, but it introduces a number of key aspects that would shape the mission and ministry of Jesus and therefore the Church and believers today. Women were to be valued and recognized for the service and servanthood they brought to the fellowship of the faithful. Healing was to be afforded in equal measure, and separation of the genders would not be tolerated or encouraged. Jesus would be seen to be just and fair, caring and compassionate to friend and stranger alike. On this occasion a simple gesture of offering the hand of healing was sufficient, and Peter's mother-in-law was able to complete her duties in the home.

The purpose of this book is to attempt, using reader-response methods, to learn the reaction of those who witnessed or attended a miracle performed by Jesus, as described in scripture. In this case we can take the position of Peter, Andrew, James, John (or Peter's wife?) to imagine our response and reaction to the miracle of the mother-in-law's healing.

What would the response look like if viewed from the absent Peter's mother-in-law's daughter, Peter's wife? If this was Simon Peter's house then surely his wife would have greater status than her mother? The problem here is that we might apply 21st century understanding to a 1st century context and culture. But in the absence of knowledge and understanding what else is possible? So for a while let us engage a degree of imagination based on our shared understanding of truth as we now view it.

Peter in the doghouse

Earlier in the day, Peter's wife had said farewell to her husband as he left for work with his brother. It was a busy day ahead as preparations for the Sabbath meal had to be complete by 3.00 p.m. to ensure that no work would be done after sunset. It had been decided that the family would have fish stew, bread and some fruit. The marketplace was unusually busy that morning, and it took a little longer to get all the provisions that were needed – but no matter because Mum was at home and she could help if time became short. Dad was not about anymore, and Mum appreciated the kindness offered to her by her son-in-law.

As the wife returns home from the market laden with the shopping, she immediately knows something is wrong as there is no sound coming from the kitchen. Her mother is always busying herself with washing-up or preparing vegetables, but there is an eerie silence in the house. Dropping the bags she goes into her mother's room and is shocked to find her in bed hardly able to lift her eyes and squeaking out an apologetic whimper that she has not been able to get up and start the housework. Assuring her not to concern herself about the chores, the wife immediately worries about the day she now has ahead of her. First things first – to make mum more comfortable; and there is no better remedy than a bowl of chicken soup. Mum had always given it to her when illness struck. Sitting her up and trying to get her to drink was not going to be easy as she was struggling to hold anything down. Sure enough, after the first attempt, the bedding had to be changed and Mum helped into fresh nightclothes; perhaps water would be a better remedy?

By midday the fish stew is still not prepared and mother's condition does not appear to be getting much better. The wife takes the difficult decision to leave Mum to sleep, hoping that her condition gets no worse, as she now needs to get Sabbath preparations under way before her husband and brother-in-law return. She works at great pace to undertake the million and one jobs necessary to create the right atmosphere for the holy day about to start. The boys will be home around 7.00 p.m. and everything must be in place – otherwise she will receive criticism and a scolding. With little time to spare, the tasks are completed and there is chance to care for Mum, who still looks very poorly.

No worry though as Peter will be home soon and he will be able to advise.

By 8.00 p.m. there is still no sign of the wayward and errant males. The service is always finished by 6.45, and it only takes five minutes to walk home from the synagogue. At first the wife had patiently awaited their arrival but that period has long since passed. She has passed the worry stage and believes they have stopped somewhere on the way home and have 'got chatting', as she knows they will say. All this time the smell of simmering fish stew has wafted through the house and Mum has been complaining about not feeling well. To say the wife is getting annoyed is an understatement, and when Peter and Andrew eventually come excitedly through the door announcing that they have brought guests and would it be alright if they stay for the seder...

It is difficult for me to describe the next conversation between Peter and his wife, but the language is neither Greek nor Aramaic! In hushed stilted and spat sentences, she delivers her verdict on the untimely and selfish actions of her husband. She does not care whether one of the guests is Yahweh himself; does he realize what sort of day she has experienced?

Witnessing the exchange Jesus knows that this would be a good time to intervene and help calm the situation. On hearing about the sick mother-in-law he goes to her room and touches her hand. The next thing anyone knows is that the fever has passed and the wife has an extra pair of hands to cope with the unexpected guests. How long it took for Peter to be let out of the 'doghouse' only he and his wife know.

The story that the reader wishes to imagine may be different, but there must be a framework that contains elements of accepted cultural norms to ensure the whims of fancy do not overtake the meaning of the text. What we are trying to achieve is a sense of the forgotten, hidden or ignored voice that must be present but has not yet found an audience. In the following chapters we shall try to discover how Jesus' healing miracles healed those who witnessed, attended and participated despite not receiving direct healing themselves.

Before we explore another of the miracles it is right to comment on the many passages which will not be considered, as they are general in nature and 'catch-all' in practice. For instance, the evening after Peter's mother-in-law's healing we are told that the whole city gathered around the door for Jesus to heal the sick with various diseases and cast out many demons (Mark 1:32-34). The villagers brought the possessed and the incurables and Jesus took upon him the infirmities and bore the diseases (Matthew 8:16-17). The demons were even heard to be shouting, "You are the Son of God," but Jesus rebuked them and would not allow them to speak (Luke 4:40-41).

There are a number of passages where Jesus is said to be healing the sick. Often these healings are tactile, whether by the people touching the fringe of his cloak [18] or by Jesus reaching out and touching the person. Demons on the other hand are rarely touched; Jesus chooses to cast them out by audible command.

The complete list of the passages that recall general healings is as follows:

- Mark 1:32-34 and 6:53-56
- Matthew 8:16-17, 14:34-36, 4:23-25, 9:35, 12:15, 14:14, 15:30, 19:1-2
- Luke 4:40-41, 5:15, 9:11

There are also passages that attest to the healings that Jesus performed in Mark 15:31, Matthew 11:2-5 and 21:13ff as well as passages where Jesus sends people out with authority to heal, Matthew 10:1ff and Luke 10:1ff

Keith Nickle, commenting on Luke 4:31-44, writes:

> *The basic issue to which the miracle stories spoke was not one of pastoral interest in the Christian solution to human calamity. The basic issue was theological: Who controls creation? Who rules in the created order?* [19]

Similarly John Proctor concludes:

> *These healings speak of mercy in a world that is often hindered and blinkered by misfortune. There is a smell of the future about*

---

[18] Deuteronomy 22:12 and Numbers 15:38, a fringe of twisted threads attached to the bottom edge of men's cloaks to draw attention to piety and remind the people of God's law

[19] Nickle, Keith F. *Preaching the Gospel of Luke: Proclaiming God's Royal Rule.* Louisville, Kentucky: Westminster John Knox Press, 2000. p45.

them. They hint at the final purposes of God and link all that to the coming Jesus, in whom God was truly 'with us' in flesh and in love. [20]

We are given a glimpse at the healing miracles through the pages of the scriptures in order to encourage us. As previously stated above, John's crescendo of hope is evident when he affirms that "Jesus did many other signs in the presence of his disciples, which are not written in this book. But these are written so that you may come to believe that Jesus is the Messiah, the Son of God and that through believing you may have life in his name." (John 20:31)

As we seek to recover the meaning and place of healing miracles in Jesus' ministry, I hope we can be encouraged and empowered as a result. We are not trying to shift from fact to fiction or from history to legend or myth, but we are attempting to learn something from the many voices hitherto unable to speak. The problem with the historical and literary criticisms of the recent past is that they have made understanding scripture an academic exercise rather than a living, endorsing, enactment for our faith today.

As Eric Eve points out:

...there seems to be rather more going on than the cure of an individual sufferer's disease. [None] of these stories need to be read as straightforward transcripts of actual historical happenings. The point is rather that they contain elements relating to the healing of illness... [21]

There is much more to the miracle stories that can inform us in our unique context and direct us toward the place of confidence and hope that Jesus' miracles are effective now.

Let's journey together into another story and learn how there is *healing beyond the miracle!*

---

[20] Proctor, John. *The People's Bible Commentary: Matthew.* Oxford: The Bible Reading Fellowship, 2001. p79.

[21] Eve, Eric. *The Healer from Nazareth: Jesus' miracles in historical context.* London: SPCK, 2009. p58.

CHAPTER TWO

She's Bleeding Dead!

Although some have tried to give a chronological ordering to Jesus' healing miracles – and there is an example in Appendix Two – such categorising is unnecessary as each healing miracle is independent and does not need support from another. Nevertheless all three synoptic gospel writers sandwich two miracles: one involving a twelve-year-old girl suffering to death; the other involving a woman plagued by haemorrhaging for twelve years. In each telling of the story, the woman's story is the 'sandwich filling' and the girl's is the outer layer.

It was the treatment of these miracles that alerted me to the excitement of reader-response criticism as a way of hearing the unheard voices from the text when Revd. Peter McIntosh led Bible study at a West Midlands Synod meeting of the United Reformed Church in 2008. He started by asking the assembly to call out an example of Jesus' healing miracles and was not surprised when someone offered the story of the woman with menstrual issue. He has since explained that this was often the miracle that groups choose when he led similar sessions during many healing weekends at Crowhurst Healing Centre near Battle, where he was Senior Chaplain from 2003 - 2008. He would then ask people to recall what they knew about the story without reference to text. It showed and validated the knowledge that people possess without realising it and encouraged people to value their own views on the meaning and purpose of scripture.

Before we delve into the substance of the miracles it will be helpful to understand the position of each Gospel writer in telling the story in the slightly different manner that they do. There is urgency within Mark's writings and a lot of movement and travel. He seems desperate to get the reader to accept his opening claim that Jesus Christ, the Son of God, is the beginning of the Good News. The gospel is presented in breathless form and miracles are evidently important, as 209 verses of the 666 contained in the book are stories and summaries about the miraculous actions of Jesus. In fact, half of the first ten chapters of Mark's gospels concentrate on Jesus' miracle stories, twenty in all, of which fourteen are healings and exorcisms. We could summarise Mark's purpose for concentrating on the miracles as primarily to encourage his readers in their faith, evangelism and life together.

I accept the weight of academic opinion that gives primacy to Mark's gospel and agree that Matthew and Luke use Mark's gospel in their own writings together with other source materials that were not available to Mark. John, written much later, is a theological reflection on the coming and second coming of Jesus, which we will say more about below when we concentrate of one of his miracle stories.

If Mark is concerned about faith, evangelism and life together, then Matthew concentrates on discipleship and the centrality of Christ as the author of faith and belief. Matthew's miracle stories are marked by the way in which the writer takes each story and shortens the detail in order to extend the discussion. In other words, Matthew wants the reader to learn the lesson from the miracle and not just marvel at the action. In telling the story Matthew wants the disciples to understand so that they in turn are able to teach the followers. Many of the healing miracles are restricted to chapters 8 and 9 where seven of the twelve are recorded. However, Matthew has many more references to general healings than the other two writers, with eight references to Jesus healing those who followed him (see Chapter One).

Dr. Luke often gives more intimate detail and shows greater pastoral concern for the patient, but he writes as one slightly removed from the original group and is therefore more reliant on other sources for the detail of the stories. His retelling of the miracle is much closer to Mark's version with additions. For example, we learn from Luke's account (22:49-51) that Malchus (name supplied by John 18:10-11), the slave of the High Priest, loses his right ear at the arrest of Jesus in the Garden of Gethsemane. Only in Luke's gospel do we learn that Jesus restores the lost lobe. As Twelftree says, "...few studies have focused on Luke's overall treatment of the miracles of Jesus." [22] Perhaps there is a study to be done to learn what the purpose and emphasis should be when reading Luke's account of the miracle stories?

So much for our brief excursion; let us return to the story of Jairus' daughter and the woman with issue of blood. What do we know without turning to the text?

- The number twelve appears significant, as it was the girl's age and the number of years that the woman had been afflicted.
- Touch is important as the woman stretched out to touch the hem of Jesus' cloak, and Jesus takes the little girl by the hand.
- There is something about delay, patience and persistence, contrasting the two stories.
- Much has previously been written (and preached) about the need of acceptance and the ways in which the woman is marginalised in this story.

When we open the scriptures we learn that Matthew (9:18-19, 20-22, 23-26) is able to tell the two stories in just nine verses: Jairus is not named; the daughter is already dead; the woman who touches the cloak is dealt with in only three verses and there is no search for her, and very little interplay between the characters occurs. However Matthew concludes the episode by saying that "[a] report of this spread throughout that district", which neither of the other two accounts add.

There are many people witnessing, observing and participating in this/these stories, and as the reader you are encouraged to find the person that you believe may have received a *healing beyond the miracle(s)*. As a church pastor and leader, I am going to take a closer look at Jairus. I have a not-so-little girl but can empathise with his feelings. What follows is an account of imagination in order that I

---

[22] Ibid., p144.

can experience the miracle and gain the effect of seeing my daughter come back to life. (I hope I have not spoiled the ending?)

This was a day like no other when I experienced the very height of joy after a deep trough of despair. My tears have flowed for most of the day, but they have turned from sorrow into wild elation. I have never lacked faith (which is just as well being the leader of the synagogue here in Capernaum) but I never expected – could never have expected – and still can't quite believe what has happened.

For almost two weeks – twelve days to be precise – my little girl had been very unwell and getting worse. She was running a high temperature and confined to her bed drifting in and out of sleep. I am fortunate to be able to afford the best physicians, but none of them had been able to cure her. Their inability should not surprise me really; we lost her mum, my wife, twelve years ago after childbirth because the doctors were unable to help. My little girl means everything to me as she is the precious link that has bound us together with the mother she has never had. We have grown together, and I have been both her mother and father for all these years.

I cannot tell you how many times in the last twelve days I knelt at the altar to pray to Yahweh to release my little girl from the illness that held her. I offered sacrifice and penitence for the sins that I had committed and pleaded that the Lord God Almighty would forgive me and my daughter for the wrongs that he held against us. Nothing happened and my little girl grew weaker. The local women spoke of a curse that was on the family, and I could imagine them saying, "First his wife and now his daughter; what has he done that the Lord God punishes him in such a way?"

It was pointless protesting my innocence as the people in Capernaum are quick to pass judgement and swift to put people out of the village if suspected of breaking the Torah. I realized I would probably be rejected myself and stripped of my leadership role in the synagogue following my little girl's illness.

There was a new man who had recently visited the area, and he was gaining quite a reputation as a healer and miracle worker. I was present when he preached in the synagogue and a worshipper called out to him. We were astounded with the authority with which he preached and amazed at the exorcism he performed. I heard that he even healed the fisherman's mother-in-law and had been criss-crossing the lake over the past few weeks. Someone said he was due back in port that very day. With my little girl now close to death he was my last hope!

I hurried down to the quayside and struggled to get through the crowd that had already gathered to greet him from the boat. People were saying that the man had been to the region of Gerasenes but had been asked to leave following an incident with a naked man who lived among the gravestones and a herd of pigs. I wasn't really interested as I was desperate to plead with the healer to come and help my little girl. I caught sight of him and managed to get in front of him. It wasn't the wisest thing to do given my status in the synagogue, but my little girl was almost gone. I fell to my knees and began to beg the man to come to my house and help make my little girl well. My pleading worked and he agreed to come with me. I jumped up and, pushing against the crowd, began to lead the way. My heart leaped as I tried to navigate a path to my little girl's bedside with the man who would soon make everything all right.

But when I looked around he had stopped and was searching for something or someone. My heart sank as I knew there was no time to lose. Just as I thought everything would be OK, another obstacle was being placed in the path, and it was becoming too much to bear. What was the hold up now?

"Someone has touched his cloak," a bystander explained.

I heard his followers explaining to the healer that there were so many pressing in on him that it was impossible to ascertain who had touched his cloak, but the man was adamant and stood motionless, asking again, "Who touched my clothes; for I noticed that power went out of me?"

I didn't know whether to laugh or cry. Here was my last hope of seeing my little girl made well and he had stopped to find out who had touched his blessed garment. I was impatient and agitated – ready to burst with rage – but the man waited until eventually a woman stepped forward. I couldn't see who she was, and the crowd were straining to hear what was being said.

I couldn't hear the entire exchange of words, but the man finished by saying, "My daughter, your faith has made you well; go in peace and be healed of your disease."

How I wished I might hear the man say these words over my daughter, and maybe I would for we started on our way again. Not long now and the man would be at my house. Just as a positive sense of wellbeing was about to come over me, some members of the synagogue who were looking after my little girl joined us and said that she had died.

My world emptied in the time it took for that sentence to be delivered. My years of faithful service were condensed into a worthless and futile expression of hopeless grief. I became numb and the world around me stopped. The colour drained from every pigment of nature and my surroundings; the outlook took on an appearance of grey. My pace slowed to nothing, and even the garden snails were overtaking me. I had lost my wife and now my daughter; there was nothing, nobody left. In that split second I had no reason to live and no wish to continue. I had reached the bottom and there was no further place to fall. I wanted to curl up and wished all the people around me would go away and leave me to drown in the tears that were now flooding from my eyes.

In the distance, cutting through my confusion, came words from the man: "Do not fear, only believe..."

This became the turning point of my whole life. I thought that I had faith but had spent all my time denying God as loving and caring. I had made my God a God of judgement, needing to be appeased and pleased; needing sacrifice and penitence rather than worship and glory. My God had become the law and the interpretation of the Scribes and Pharisees. There was no room for a gracious, loving and compassionate God, and I had led others to view God in the same way. We had become good at fearing God at the expense of loving Him and accepting Him as the author and creator of our being. With those words, "Do not fear, only believe," my world changed.

The next thing I knew was a hand being placed into mine and helping me to stand. It was a familiar hand but one that I hadn't felt for many years. It was tender and kind, soft and strong. I wiped away the tears only for them to well up again as I caught sight of the one helping me to my feet. After all this time was it possible, could it really be, or was I just dreaming?

"The bleeding has stopped," she said. "I can come back home now."

It was my wife, returned to me after twelve long years of separation. Following the birth of our little girl, she had been forced to live apart from us because she remained unclean for all that time. She was not allowed into the village and was estranged from us while trying to affect a cure. Despite all she had endured under many physicians and despite all the money we had spent finding a cure, we had never expected this day to come.

"I touched the man's cloak and was healed," she said. "Come, let's see our daughter together."

As we arrived home, the flute players and wailers were in attendance and the funeral rites had started. The congregation were trying to help by showing their loving support and getting the ceremony prepared to save me the agony.

The man simply told them all to leave, as our little girl was not dead but sleeping. The people didn't believe him and started to laugh, but he knew. He took us into the bedroom with a couple of his followers and took our little girl by the hand quietly, saying, "Get up."

She did, and the three of us cried and cried and cried until the man told us to have some food and not say a word about what had happened – but how do you keep something like this a secret?

In the story, none of the scriptural facts have been changed, and in fact many of the words spoken by Jesus are reprinted. There is nothing to say that the woman and Jairus are linked, but all three synoptic writers choose to combine their stories. There is no other healing sandwich of this type in any of the Gospels. There are other miracle sandwiches in Mark, but this is the only time that the three writers offer two healing stories in this manner. Even if the characters only share the canvas, is it wrong to allow them other common features? Does the story I have told only offer a flight of fancy? It has been used to help understand how the daughter's healing miracle was a healing story for the father. The mother only appears at the end of the story, and we get little understanding of her feeling and emotions. Even the father is displayed as a reactive character within the miracle.

Scripture rarely provides us with the sense of grief, sadness, relief and joy displayed by the people whose story it is. This book seeks to redress that in order to capture, not just the feelings and emotions,

41

but the purpose and essence of the event for our living today. I am attempting to use imaginative writing in order to hear a new voice. On this occasion we are trying to understand what led a first century synagogue leader to call upon a visiting miracle worker and healer as a last attempt to save his daughter, and within the story we learn of another cure. As Twelftree points out:

> Given that there were many sick people in Palestine and given that he was a successful and sought-after healer, we can assume that Jesus made some choices about whom he healed and the kind of miracles he performed. [23]

Even if we subscribe to the view that Jesus healed many others, we are still left to ponder why the writers chose to record these miracles which we now study. Why were these particular stories handed onto us, and how are they meant to encourage us today?

Numbers 5 and Leviticus 15 tell us that the woman threatened the purity of the camp and anyone touching her, or touched by her, would be equally unclean. We know that under *Tumat HaMet* [24] there are many restrictions when touching the dead, and yet Jesus ignores all this weight of Torah in order to bring about cure and healing. This fact was surely not lost on Jairus given his role as leader in the synagogue.

In your reading you may wish to consider the message as referring more to the new law Jesus brings in seeing the person and their needs, rather than the ordinances and restrictions of the law. Rather than worry about ritual contamination, Jesus is a virus of compassion and love. His power is to be taken as well as be given, and he is ready to overturn the taboos of his day.

As we consider the *healing beyond the miracle* for today, what do we need to amend in our attitudes in order to effect change and bring about cure?

---

[23] Ibid., p 262.
[24] "The impurity of death" and the requirements for purification following contact with a dead body

CHAPTER THREE

Don't drop me

I was a roofer once, before the accident, earning good money and going places. I had it all: the wealth; the wife and family; the status in the community; all the trappings of a successful businessman. If you had seen me, confined to my bed from day-to-day with nothing to do but stare at the ceiling... My paralysis meant that I couldn't even feel pain, apart from the emotional and spiritual damage deep within. The money was almost gone and my family left me. I was an anonymous nobody wasting away with no future. If I had been able to lift a hand I would have struck myself down. I was not even able to thank the four friends who remained loyal to me, dropping in and out during the day to make sure I was comfortable and well refreshed in every manner (if you understand my meaning).

My four friends were all employed in the business and have remained with me despite my incapacity. Tertius was my bookkeeper and made sure the office was well run and all the accounts kept up to date. He is great at letter-writing and attends to all the correspondence and administration. I wouldn't be able to survive if it weren't for him. Erastus was my second in command, and I had considered making him a partner before I fell from that roof in Capernaum. He could be trusted to get on with the work and always finished the job on time and on budget. He ensures that my current shelter is well maintained – and again, I wouldn't be able to survive if it weren't for him.

My third friend is Gaius, and he has a special quality of hospitality that shines through whenever he visits. By trade he is a thatcher, and I used him regularly to help make a roof watertight, but I think his greater gift is making those around him welcome and comfortable. Nothing is ever too much trouble, and he can be relied upon to provide refreshment to any who visit. He is so attentive to my needs that I wouldn't be able to survive if it weren't for him. Finally there's Jason, a big man but gentle as they come and absolutely trustworthy and loyal. You can depend on Jason to get you out of any tight situation. His very size stops people from challenging, but even if he needed to take on a crowd, he would for his friends. He was my labourer and is now a regular visitor to help me since the accident. I wouldn't be able to survive if it weren't for him.

I am very lucky to have four such good friends, and my previous actions mean that I really don't deserve to have them. I have wronged each one at different times: holding back wages or docking them the bonus they were due because I was greedy and wanted to keep the money. I had a quick temper and lashing tongue when we worked together and yet they remain friends. On the day of the accident, Erastus warned me that the materials I had acquired on the cheap were sub-standard and we shouldn't use them. Gaius had winced when he saw the materials and refused to go up onto the roof with me. He said it was dangerous and so did Jason. I knew best and after berating them for their lack of faith I climbed the ladder and crept out onto the eaves. They were right; I fell to the ground breaking many bones and becoming paralysed from the neck down.

It was my own fault. I should have listened, but I knew best as I always did. I have thought about that day many times since the accident and reflected on the numerous occasions in my life when I have made wrong and even bad choices. Is it any wonder that everyone has left me and I don't really understand why the four friends remain?

Jason was chatting about a new guy in town called Jesus who was creating quite a stir. I'm not sure whether Jason knows that I can hear him as I am unable to respond beyond a wink and a slight twitch here and there, but he chunters on regardless. He was saying that he preached in the local synagogue so well that people were listening. I smiled inside knowing that they wouldn't find me in that place even when I was well. All those scribes telling me how to live. What do they know? They have never done a day's work in their lives. Jason went on to say something about a demon possessing one of the people there and Jesus managing to cast it out. It must have been quite a sight because by the next evening loads of the villagers had congregated around Peter and Andrew's house hoping that this Jesus could heal them.

I knew the fishermen from the past as I had done some work on that very roof. Erastus and I had done a good job on that house, and we were hoping for some repeat business one day. Jason reckoned that Jesus had cured Peter's mother-in-law. I wish he could have read my thoughts and shared the joke I was having at the sound of that news. I know what I would like to do with my mother-in-law and it wouldn't be as considerate. Jason finished what he was doing and left. Later in the day Tertius came to sort out some paperwork and spoke about the same thing as Jason. Clearly Jesus had made an impression on my friends, but I was still surprised a couple of days later when all four arrived and started carrying me through the streets. What were they doing, I wondered?

We arrived at the fishermen's house but couldn't enter because of the crowd that had gathered. I could see my four friends deep in conversation, and what happened next frightened the life out of me. They climbed the stairs to the right of the house and carried me to the roof. Erastus set Gaius and Jason to work on making a hole in the thatch while he and Tertius held on to my bed. "Don't drop me," I thought. They carefully lowered me down until leaders from the synagogue and the village surrounded me. I was in the middle of the lower ground floor. I had crashed in on a heavy conversation that they were having with a man who I later found out was Jesus.

Everything went silent for what seemed an age...

Then Jesus looked at me and started to speak. I missed the first few words. It was something like, "Take heart, son (or friend)," but the next sentence was unmistakeable: "Your sins are forgiven." I remained motionless, thinking about what Jesus had said and began to recall all the things in my life that had led to this point: all the dodgy deals; the unfaithfulness toward friends; the apathy toward God; and the challenging behaviours that I often displayed to others. Jesus had said that these were all forgiven. I no longer needed to hold onto the hurt inside and dwell on the damage I had done to others. I was free to live again. While these thoughts raced around in my mind Jesus

45

seemed to be having an intense conversation with the religious people. He looked at me again and this time said, "Stand up, take your bed and go home." So I did. I stood up, picked up my bed and went home. As I walked away people were astonished and saying that they had just seen a strange thing happen, something that they had never seen before. The crowd stayed on to applaud Jesus and listen to him further, but I went home hoping to find Tertius, Gaius, Erastus and Jason in order to celebrate my good fortune and their deep friendship.

Over the years since this incident the five of us have travelled in different directions but our friendship remains strong and we have each decided to serve Jesus in our own way. Tertius has become a secretary to an evangelist called Paul, Erastus is a city director of works in Rome, where Gaius runs a Christian retreat house and Jason has a home in Thessalonica. As for me I am still a roofer, and yes I did repair the fishermen's thatch, it was the first job I completed on my return to work.

Okay, so I may have stretched the licence a little far in giving the friends the names of other characters that later appear in the Acts of the Apostles and writings of Paul. However, I wanted to illustrate how we can use a reader-response critical approach to a well-known story to imagine *the healing beyond the miracle.*

When we consider this story as recorded in scripture, the scribes and Pharisees interpreted Jesus' actions so very wrongly. The temple officials were so concerned about the forgiveness of sin that they were not interested in the actual healing. On the other hand, the people were amazed at the healing and nonplussed about the forgiveness being granted. The paralytic's reaction after being forgiven was to lie still, giving the appearance that nothing had happened. It is only when the man stands up that the effect of the healing is realised.

In Mark's gospel this is the first miracle that indicates the later opposition to come. The writer is the only one to set it in Capernaum, and as it follows the previous miracles it can be argued that the home to which it refers is that owned by Peter and Andrew. In typical style, Matthew condenses the story to half the number of verses of the other two writers and leaves out the episode of the friends lowering the bed through the roof. Luke uses a slightly different word for the man's affliction, but all agree that he was unable to care for himself.

The essence of this miracle is the connection between sin and illness, and the purpose of Jesus' healing is to teach something of this to the religious leaders and the crowd that gathered. The beneficiary was the paralysed man, but I also think there were numerous others who received healing as a result of the miracle. What did they learn?

Sin and illness were inextricably linked in the minds of the religious faithful. The psalmist writes:

Psalms 32:1-11

Happy are those whose transgression is forgiven, whose sin is covered. Happy are those to whom the LORD imputes no iniquity and in whose spirit there is no deceit. While I kept silence, my body wasted away through my groaning all day long. For day and night your hand was heavy upon me; my strength was dried up as by the heat of summer. Then I acknowledged my sin to you and I did not hide my iniquity; I said, "I will confess my transgressions to the LORD," and you forgave the guilt of my sin. Therefore, let all who are faithful offer prayer to you; at a time of distress, the rush of mighty waters shall not reach them. You are a hiding place for me; you preserve me from trouble; you surround me with glad cries of deliverance. I will instruct you and teach you the way you should go; I will counsel you with my eye upon you. Do not be like a horse or a mule, without understanding, whose temper must be curbed with bit and bridle, else it will not stay near you. Many are the torments of the wicked, but steadfast love surrounds those who trust in the LORD. Be glad in the LORD and rejoice, O righteous and shout for joy, all you upright in heart.

This psalm is almost certainly written by David after his great sin with Bathsheba recorded in 2 Samuel 11 and 12. It connects with the many offering requirements of Leviticus 1-7 in response to sin and guilt. When we add to these the chronicling of good and bad kings following the death of Solomon and the cry of the people in exile from the second temple, we begin to understand how the people interpreted sin as the cause of disease, illness and demon possession. We can evidence this further from questions put to Jesus regarding the cause of people's illness – John 9:2 for instance (see Chapter Four) and we can make a convincing case that the people of the time saw illness as proof of the person's guilty sin.

A link through the computer online dictionary led me to this statement about sin as viewed from a modern Jewish perspective.

Hebrew has several words for sin, each with its own specific meaning. The word *pesha* ('trespass') means a sin done out of rebelliousness. The word *aveira* means 'transgression'. And the word *avone* ('iniquity') means a sin done out of moral failing. The word most commonly translated simply as 'sin', *het*, literally means 'to go astray'. Just as Jewish law, *halakha*, provides the proper 'way' (or path) to live, sin involves straying from that path. [25]

The sense that people have strayed from the path suits the purpose of the story we have considered above. It is a catchall term that does not mean that the person is necessarily guilty of a huge crime or is wicked or evil but has slipped from the perfection that being one of God's chosen people demands. We are equally as guilty of this, and all fall short of perfection. This would not come as any great surprise to most of the readers today, but in the context and setting of 1st century Roman-occupied Capernaum, a reason for such malaise might well have been one of non-religious observance.

Today we can accept the death and resurrection of Jesus as the proof for our forgiveness. The characters in the story had no such luxury. For them the option of the priest was still there but required the various offering outlined in scripture – and there was still no guarantee of a pardon. One might sympathise with the Pharisee and scribes in their attempt to keep good order and encourage God's followers to lead blameless and fulfilled lives, but this was impossible then as now, particularly with the weight of Torah and Mishnah with which to contend. If Jesus was a false prophet they must follow the instruction in Deuteronomy 13 and put him to death, but since they can neither heal the sick nor forgive sin as he has demonstrated, what are they to do? Another Psalm (103) tells them to "Praise the Lord – who forgives all your sins and heals all your diseases." What an opportunity they missed when they came to the meeting with a critical spirit instead of a repentant heart! Whenever we consider those who experience *healing beyond the miracle* we are always going to leave out those who did not understand and whose ears were closed to the possibility of hearing God's Good News.

---

[25] Wikipedia: Jewish views on sin. Accessed via Apple Dictionary on 080611

The paralytic received a two-fold healing on the day his friends brought him to Jesus. The first was forgiveness for the sins he had committed and the second for the paralysis that bound him. When Revd. Peter McIntosh led the West Midlands Synod in Bible study he asked people to call out words for healing. The responses were: release, acceptance, renewal, reconciliation, change, intervention, cure, *shalom*, anointing, restoration, loving, caring, wholeness, therapy, salvation, balance, confession and death. He concluded that illness robs people of their wholeness. Sin equally robs people of wholeness, as the separation from God is a separation from the created order and the creator's orders. So what do we mean by being healed?

The Greek dictionary gives us three quite different words that are translated 'healed' in English Bibles:

- *Therapeua – θεραπεύω*
  From which we derive the word therapeutic, therapy and therapist. The original word meant 'to dress wounds, to tend the sick and dying, to wash, to care for, do service and to treat medically.' By extension it means curing, healing and restoring to health.

- *Iaomai – ἰάομαι*
  Similar to 'therapeua' but a word for healing, curing and making whole, more often used within the medical profession. It enlarged its meaning to include 'curing from errors and sins and bringing about one's salvation'.

- *Sozo – σώζω*
  The last of the three verbs is again a word whose origin predates the New Testament meaning 'to make sound, to save, to preserve safe from danger, loss, or destruction'. Taken into Christian usage its meaning was enlarged to 'saving from death, judgment and bringing in all positive blessings in the place of condemnation', i.e. salvation.

Returning to the story of the paralytic, Jesus never pronounced a healing but infers it in his two-fold cure. At first he tells the man his sins are forgiven and then tells him to stand up. By his physical movement we can be witness to the second healing, but it will be only by his later actions that we will have any clue as to whether the first can be proven.

We could argue that the paralytic was primarily healed from within when his spirit was brought into an accord with Jesus and then secondarily he was healed from without and his physical state was repaired to enable him to witness to the first. What scripture rarely tells us is the result of Jesus' healing miracles beyond the event – how the person went on to live their life. If we knew that then trying to imagine how the miracle affected others would be easier and would guide the modern reader in viewing the stories, but we do not have that information so we are trying to use an approach that will encourage and guide us in our present day living.

Sin is around and within the human condition, and we are always short of the perfection that God desires. Stanley Hauerwas recaptures the link between sin and sickness believing "sickness to be a manifestation of sin". He continues:

> *Alcoholics discover they are possessed by a power they do not remember choosing but for which they must take responsibility if they are to stand any chance of being free from the possession. In like manner Christians confess that they are sinners. Sin, like sickness, seems more like something that happens to us than what we do. Yet as Christians we believe we are rightly held accountable for our sins.* [26]

He argues that we are atheists, even if we say we believe in God, by the way in which we order our lives. He evidences this by asking people how they wish to die and the response is invariably: quick, painlessly and in my sleep, not being a burden to others. In the past people would want to ensure they were reconciled with their neighbour, church and God and would therefore be horrified by a sudden death. He concludes that we no longer fear the judgment of God but fear death itself and order our lives to reflect this change. Sickness becomes the reminder of death, and so we go to the doctor to take away our symptoms and restore us to wellbeing. "Put bluntly," Hauerwas says, "we are unable to make sense of our being

---

[26] Braaten, Carl E. & Jenson Robert W. (Ed). *Sin, Death and the Devil.* Grand Rapids, Michigan: William B Eerdmans Publishing Co., 2000. p 8

sick because we no longer understand what it means for our lives to be captured by sin." [27]

The force of his argument is that we are captured by sin rather than guilty of it. As sin lurks around us, it is ready to take over our lives and create the disease that is manifest in sickness and human decay. Hauerwas suggests that illness is embraced as an opportunity to witness the new creation that is in advance of us. This is beyond the scope of this book but it points towards the *healing beyond the miracle* of the paralytic's reparation. As he stood up, took up his bed and walked out of that roof-damaged home, his four friends, the scribes and Pharisees, the onlookers and the disciples and followers, had just witnessed a glimpse of how Jesus was to restore God's people despite their feckless behaviour. We might wonder and reflect on who received this *healing beyond the miracle* and whether we equally receive such healing today?

---

[27] Ibid., p 10

CHAPTER FOUR

My eyes are dim, I cannot see

There are a number of miracles that involve the healing of blind men (sic) recorded in all four Gospels. Mark records the story of the man of Bethesda (8:22-26) and Bartimaeus (10:46-52). This is one of the few occasions where the person being healed is named, and we could develop this further (see Chapter Eleven). Matthew appears to tell the Bartimaeus story twice but setting the miracle as the healing of two blind men (without naming either) in the passages 9:27-31 and 20:29-34. This is not the only place where Matthew records a story using two characters instead of one employed by Mark and Luke. It is possible that Matthew does this to add emphasis to the story, validating it with a witness one to the other. The writer also records another healing involving a blind, mute demoniac (12:22-32). Luke repeats Mark's version of Bartimaeus' healing in 18:35-43 without naming him and records a similar version of Matthew's healing of the blind and mute demoniac at 11:14-23.

We start, however, with John's third recorded healing miracle of the man born blind, upon which he reflects thoroughly in his writings (9:1-41). John's version is one of six miracles where the parents of the recipients are also involved. The other five are:

- John 4   Healing the nobleman's son at Cana
- Luke 7   Raising the widow's son at Cain
- Mark 5 et al.   Raising Jairus' daughter in Capernaum
- Mark 7/Mat 5   Delivering the Syrophoenician's daughter
- Mark 9 et al.   Delivering the demon-possessed boy

The clear implication in Deuteronomy 24:16 ("Parents shall not be put to death for their children, nor shall children be put to death for their parents; only for their own crimes may persons be put to death.") makes the question put by the disciples in John 9:1-2 a nonsense question. The later interrogation of the parents by the Pharisee indicates that they were not prepared to do their utmost in support of Jesus, rather deferring the question to the son who was old enough to speak for himself. His response was, however, bold and in emphatic support of Jesus as the miracle worker who restored his sight. In fact, we can observe the revelatory progression given to the blind man by the Holy Spirit regarding the person of Jesus.

- 9:11   he calls him a man
- 9:17   he calls him a prophet
- 9:23   he calls him a messenger from God
- 9:32   he calls him a miracle worker
- 9:35-38   he worships him as the Son of God

There are different views as to which of the miracles are parallels in the synoptic Gospels of Matthew, Mark and Luke; suffice to say in this study, healing the blind had significance to those who witnessed the event.

Because we are more concerned at getting to the *healing beyond the miracle*, we will not consider in depth the manner in which Jesus performed the healings. Others have written about the use of saliva and the double treatment that was required to affect a full recovery of sight (Mark 8:22ff). Nor will we reflect on the reference to "looking like trees walking" and the suggestion that this is being used as a metaphor for the people of God. We will consider the title 'Son of David' and the geography of the miracle as Jesus faces the fulfilment of his own ministry. As both Matthew and Luke include a discussion about the Beelzebul controversy, we will weave this into our reflection and add John's debate about the parents' sins being the reason for the man's blindness from birth. Further consideration is given to the place of sin generally in the previous chapter above.

It is argued that physical blindness was linked with spiritual blindness. Jesus quotes from Isaiah 6:9-10 to explain why he uses parables:

Matthew 13:10-17

Then the disciples came and asked him, "Why do you speak to them in parables?" He answered, "To you it has been given to know the secrets of the kingdom of heaven, but to them it has not been given. For to those who have, more will be given and they will have an abundance; but from those who have nothing, even what they have will be taken away. The reason I speak to them in parables is that 'seeing they do not perceive and hearing they do not listen, nor do they understand.' With them indeed is fulfilled the prophecy of Isaiah that says: 'You will indeed listen, but never understand and you will indeed look, but never perceive. For this people's heart has grown dull and their ears are hard of hearing and they have shut their eyes; so that they might not look with their eyes and listen with their ears and understand with their heart and turn— and I would heal them.' But blessed are your eyes, for they see and your ears, for they hear. Truly I tell you, many prophets and righteous people longed to see what you see, but did not see it and to hear what you hear, but did not hear it."

The healing miracles, similarly, have much more to say than simply that a person is cured. Each act of compassion is to be understood as a message from Jesus of greater importance to those who witnessed the event. Such an act might equally be viewed as a sign or message to us, the modern reader of the story. Not only is there a *healing beyond the miracle* for those who physically attended and witnessed the marvel but I hope the reader is beginning to understand that there is a healing for us as well. Mark retells a story to illustrate the disciples' inability to understand the significance of the feeding miracles (8:14-21). In exasperation, Jesus berates them:

Mark 8:17-18

"Do you still not perceive or understand? Are your hearts hardened? Do you have eyes and fail to see? Do you have ears and fail to hear? Do you not yet understand?"

It is not surprising that the next action in the account is that of Jesus healing the blind man of Bethesda. To affect the healing, Jesus looked intently at the man who was then able to see everything.

John suggests:

John 12:42,43
Many, even of the authorities, believed in him. But because of the Pharisees they did not confess it, for fear that they would be put out of the synagogue; for they loved human glory more than the glory that comes from God.

So even those who could see could not be persuaded to believe sufficiently to relinquish what they could touch. The eight references (I will suggest they relate to four or five different stories) to the cure of blindness each have aspects of teaching to a wider audience in order to encourage and persuade onlookers, witnesses and friends of those healed to reflect on their own vision of God through the ministry and miracles of Jesus.

The difficulty of separating the passages into independent stories or bringing them together as coherent parallels results in much hazy recollection when asking a group to say what they know about this aspect of Jesus' healing miracles. When working with groups there is often a pause as tentatively they suggest the content of the story. Some are able to recognize a multiplicity of stories, but only a few are able to confidently say which details belong to which story. Consequently the reader-response to this group of miracles involving sight and vision is already opaque. The following story may not help this process as it will be told in the form of an interview between a reporter and the parents of the man born blind in John's gospel account but will include the accusation that Jesus was in the employ of Beelzebul and that the blind man called Jesus 'the Son of David'. What I will attempt to achieve is a picture of how many others received insight as a result of the healing.

Reporter: Thank you Mr. and Mrs. Timaeus for agreeing to be interviewed following the healing of your son's blindness. Our readership is fascinated by your story and would like to know what happened. I understand your son was blind from birth; is that correct?

Mrs. T: Yes, I have lived with worry and concern that my excessive alcohol drinking while pregnant caused Bart to be born blind. Every day I have regretted every sip of wine that may have caused his disability. [A tear creeps into the corner of her eye.]

Mr. T: *Let's not get upset; he is cured and can look forward to an independent life from now on.*

Rep: *Where did the extraordinary events take place and how did it all happen?*

Mr. T: *We live just outside Jerusalem on the Jericho Road, and on Saturday morning as usual Barty sat outside listening and talking to the passers-by. He is very good at discerning who is coming and going by the sound of their footsteps. We were inside observing Sabbath on our own as most of our neighbours ignore and shun us believing that we caused Barty's blindness because of our wrongdoings – ridiculous really but what can we do? Fortunately most people are kind and generous to him.*

Mrs. T: *There was a commotion outside, and we heard Bart calling out, "Jesus, Son of David, have mercy on me!" Our son is normally very quiet and doesn't shout out. We could hear our neighbours telling him to be quiet, but that didn't stop him. If anything he shouted even louder.*

Rep: *'Son of David' is an interesting title; what was your son thinking?*

Mrs. T: *He told us later that he had heard stories about a prophet and healer who operated in the north, around Capernaum, and was creating quite a stir. Evidently this Jesus had gained a large following so Bart put two and two together when he heard the throng that were passing by and he asked the neighbour who confirmed it was Jesus. As we went out to see what was going on, Bart was on his feet and talking to him.*

Mr. T: *That was when I heard Jesus say to his followers that his parents were not to blame for Barty's blindness. I can't tell you how good that sounded. For the first time someone said what I believed – that Barty was blind because God had another purpose for him, to show others their own blindness of spirit and understanding.*

Rep: *Surely you don't think that God made your son blind do you?*

Mr. T: *No, I think that natural things caused his disability from birth, but I always knew that he would be used by God one day and hoped that this was it.*

Rep: *So what happened next?*

Mrs. T: I saw Jesus make a mudpack and place it on Bart's eyes, before telling him to walk down to the pool of Siloam. The crowd was too large for me to get to him, but when he returned he could see for the first time in his life. People wondered if it was really he, but I knew it was – and he recognized me! We hugged for a long time while all the people tried to rationalise what had just happened.

Mr. T: I began to get annoyed at the disbelief shown by the crowd and offered to take Barty to the Temple officials to prove that he had been cured. Blow me if even <u>they</u> didn't start questioning the healing! The Pharisees and scribes became fixated with the healing taking place on the Sabbath – therefore it could not be of God. They even claimed that Jesus must be an agent for Beelzebul, able to cast out demons because he was one himself. Simply asking them by whose authority do they exorcise demons seemed to answer that question. Barty came up with the best answer though when he said that he didn't know anything about Sabbaths and demons but could say that though he was blind, now he sees. His mother and I also confirmed when asked by the Pharisee that Barty was born blind but can now see clearly. Barty got very annoyed with the holy and righteous men accusing them of inner blindness. He asked them to respond, but they refused and dismissed us from the synagogue.

Mrs. T: When we got home Jesus was waiting for us. He had heard what happened in the synagogue and wanted us all to know why he had healed Bart. He said that he had come into the world as judgment so that those who do not see may see and those who do see may be blind. I admit that I do not fully understand but know that I must think upon what he did and what he said a little more. He also turned to Bart and said that his faith had saved him and made him well.

Rep: What do you think that Jesus meant by this?

Mr. T: I don't know exactly, but I believe that Jesus has come to bring good news to the poor. He has been sent to proclaim release to the captives and recovery of sight to the blind, to let the oppressed go free and to proclaim the year of the Lord's favour. I believe this is the man whom the whole nation has been waiting for.

Rep: And how do you feel?

Mrs. T: Released from the guilt I have felt for so many years. We were not punished by God and given a blind son but blessed with a child who grew up to be a man of far-sighted faith, belief and trust. Bart is an example to everyone who sees deep within and has the courage to share it with everyone, even the opponents.

Rep: Thank you, Mr. and Mrs. Timaeus, for sharing your story.

On this occasion, I have imagined a story from the blind man's parents' point of view, but there are others whom we could consider from the corpus of stories. We could be one of the "some people" at Bethesda or one of the disciples who were receiving a lesson in understanding. We could be in the crowd leaving Jericho or the Pharisee who accused Jesus.

It is possible that someone reading this today has struggled or is struggling with an understanding of why bad things happen to good people. What had the foetal child done in the womb that caused him to be blind from birth? Few would seriously accuse a developing embryo of being inherently sinful. It is no wonder that the blame is placed on the parents and often accepted more readily by the mother. We are beginning to have a better understanding of genetic disorders and defective chromosome development, which leads us to be more circumspect about apportioning blame. Nevertheless the cry of "Why me?" can still be heard on the lips of a person who does not receive the perfection that is expected.

While serving as Chaplain to a school for children, some with life limiting disabilities, I learnt that most parents are able to adjust their thinking and look upon their child as a gift, despite their many disabilities. A parent of a Downs' Syndrome child once told me that children born with the condition are like God's angels sent to teach people on earth how to love. I suspect this positive view could not be shared by all parents with Downs' Syndrome children. The question still remains, "Why do bad things happen to people?" I met a lady in a queue during the summer as we waited for three hours to see a tennis match. She was vivacious and enthusiastic and spoke of a positive mindset that she brings to every aspect of her life. A brief survey of her story is contained in a self-help personal motivation book which she handed me. [28] It shows that she was born into a wealthy family who lived on a farm and kept horses. However, their idyll was shattered when first her father committed suicide and then, six years later, her brother suffered the same fate. Her first marriage ended in divorce, and after marrying again, their first child was lost at twenty four weeks' gestation. She writes:

> *I am a survivor! Nothing stops me from how I choose to feel. I have rediscovered how to be in love with my life, in love with me and deeply grateful, always finding a way to succeed in everything, feeling grateful and feeling abundant in every area of my life, no matter what the current circumstances look like!* [29]

She has learnt to accept her situation and the context in which she lives, recognising that it will constantly change and that the only certainty in life is uncertainty. None of us can choose our future although we might try to minimize the consequences of things we can influence. Our healing does not come from being cured of disease but by the way we live with the disordering of our lives. As we bring order to the chaos that illness brings, we may not return to the former position we held. It might even release us into a place that becomes more fulfilling and nurturing than the one in which our perfect health leaves behind. I am not suggesting that we choose to be unwell, but when ill health comes we can take the option to 'give up' on life or we can find a new way of being. If the latter is possible then we might experience a degree of hindsight grace where God can be found in the healing process. Scripture assures us, "No harm happens to the righteous." (Proverbs 12:21).

If we accept that God will only send us good things, then our response to illness cannot be one of self-pity or self indulgence but of expectation for the new things about to happen. Instead of "Why me?" we might think "Why not?" Good people are not being singled out for special treatment that results in their malaise and disease, but illness happens and we can choose how we respond to the change in our circumstances. In time our life purpose is revealed and we are free to respond. Really exciting things happen when we recognise how we

---

[28] Brown, Les (Ed). Multiple Streams of Determination. (Dallas, USA: Wimbrey Training Systems, 2011), p113ff.

[29] Ibid., p116/117

can respond to God's will and use our renewed state of being to influence those around us.

This is called evangelism when we act as messengers for God, sharing the Good News that Jesus brought and, enabled by the Holy Spirit, share with others the life-giving streams of living water that satisfy even the thirstiest of (un)believers. Surely this was how the healing of the blind became a *healing beyond the miracle*, as they acted as witnesses of the vision that Jesus brings, into the loving heart of the creator God and the good things he wants us all to share?

CHAPTER FIVE

Choose to make me clean

In the Prologue I suggested that the reader cannot come to text without some knowledge or expectation. The implied reader of this book is a person who has some experience of the Christian faith and therefore reads the healing miracles of Jesus with a degree of belief. The intended reader is someone with imagination and a desire to learn something of the story that is hidden from us. The subterfuge is not deliberate or planned but a result of the way in which the original story was told in its context and culture. The writing has further been influenced and affected by translation and translators, and our understanding is guided by the sermons we have heard, the commentaries we have read and the traditions to which we adhere.

I fully accept that the style of study proposed by this work will not be acceptable to those who are heavily indebted to literary and historical criticisms for their understanding of the text. I am prepared for those who would evaluate the imaginative reader-response approach as a flimsy flight of fancy without substance or value. In response I would again draw attention to Paul's letter to Timothy, which claims, "All scripture is inspired by God and is useful." (2 Tim 3:16). Also note "that the word of God endures forever" (Isaiah 40:8 and that the psalmist writes, "The unfolding of your words gives light; it gives understanding to the simple." (Psalms 119:130). Our challenge is to be open to fresh interpretation, and one way is to accept the possibility that God is speaking through an individual's imagination. My caveat is, however, to accept that the conclusion should remain grounded in the general understanding of the Church.

It is therefore helpful and useful if a background story could be established in order to place any imaginative story within the same context. Our next two healing miracles relate to the cleansing of a leper and ten lepers, the latter only recorded by Luke.

The Hebrew word translated as *lepra* in the Greek, is *tsara'ath*. It means 'to smite or strike' and refers not only to a number of different skin diseases afflicting a person but also the mould and mildew found in fabrics and houses. The personal illness is described as follows:

> *[This disease] begins with specks on the eyelids and on the palms, gradually spreading over the body, bleaching the hair white wherever they appear, crusting the affected parts with white scales and causing terrible sores and swellings. From the skin the disease eats inward to the bones, rotting the whole body piecemeal.*
>
> *In Christ's day no leper could live in a walled town, though he might in an open village. But wherever he was he was required to have his outer garment rent as a sign of deep grief, to go bareheaded and to cover his beard with his mantle, as if in lamentation at his own virtual death. He had further to warn passers-by to keep away from him, by calling out, 'Unclean! unclean!' nor could he speak to any one, or receive or return a salutation, since in the East this involves an embrace.* [30]

Luke tells us that there were many Jews infected by the disease in the time of Elisha the prophet, but only Naaman the Syrian was healed (Luke 4:27), suggesting that it was largely an incurable condition. This is supported in the Hebrew writings by the reaction of the king of Israel when Naaman presented him with a letter from the king of Aram requesting a cure for the commander's leprosy. Later in the story we learn that the disease was passed onto Gehazi, Elisha's servant, who tried to profit from his master's success in healing Naaman. The passage suggests that the punishment would be passed down through the generations and had made Gehazi appeared 'as white as snow' (2 Kings 5).

There are two other references to people being punished by the affliction of leprosy. Miriam had questioned Moses' choice of a Cushite bride, and God punished her disloyalty by making her

---

[30] M.G. Easton, Easton's Bible Dictionary (Oak Harbor, WA: Logos Research Systems, Inc., 1996, c1897).

leprous, only to have the sanction reduced to seven days after Moses pleaded clemency for her (Numbers 12). Such leniency was not shown to Uzziah after he became too powerful, "his pride leading to his downfall". He was unfaithful to the Lord his God and entered the Temple to burn incense, a task given only to the priests of Aaron. His punishment was to contract leprosy after he refused to leave the Temple and raged at the priests who had come to confront him. He lived with the disease until the day he died in a separate house, or a house where he was relieved of all responsibilities, and his son Jotham took charge of the palace and governed the people of the land (2 Chronicles 26). It is not difficult to see how leprosy became associated with an outward and visible sign of the innermost spiritual corruption. It also rendered the person unworthy to enter the presence of a pure and holy God.

Part of the Levitical code (Leviticus 13-14) was established to give structure to the community in dealing with leprosy in order to avoid it spreading and infecting others. It is a very early version of quarantine, which incidentally is a Latin word with reference to forty days of isolation. In this case, the priest would commit a person to seven days of isolation to see if a swelling or rash displayed the telltale signs of white hair around the sore, which would confirm it to be leprosy. It was for the priest to declare whether a person was clean or unclean with some elaborate detail about different skin irritations involving the colour of the boil or rash and the later development of the condition. Interestingly, a person was deemed clean if the whole body, head to toe, was covered with the disease. The pronouncement by the priest that a person was unclean rendered them separated from the community, and as long as the infection persisted they had to live alone outside the camp. The reader might want to investigate further the criteria used for being declared clean or unclean, particularly if the reader is a bald-headed man!

The separation is significant because it meant they could not enter a place of worship, have intimate relationships, associate with others (unless they were also infected), or maintain decency (they had to let their hair be unkempt/uncovered and have their clothing ripped open). In addition they had to shout to passers-by, warning of their uncleanliness, therefore bringing further attention to themselves of their desperate situation. It is reported that such a situation moved a group of four men with leprosy who were starving to death during a siege on Samaria to take a risky action. They reckoned that they might as well let the Arameans, who were laying siege to the city, put them to death rather than stay where they were with no food. When they arrived at the Aramean camp it was deserted, and after they had their fill to eat they reported back to the city guards (from a distance, naturally) and the city survived (2 Kings 6:24-7:20). We assume the men remained leprous; therefore their action did not mean they could be reunited with the community but had to continue to be separated from their kinsfolk.

The only way to be reconciled with the community was to be healed and deemed clean by the priest who would then preside over an eight-day ceremonial service involving two living clean birds; some cedar wood, scarlet yarn and hyssop; laundering clothes, shaving hair and bathing; more shaving, but this time involving every follicle of hair on the body, seven days after sitting outside the camp in a tent; more laundering and more bathing; then on the eighth day two male lambs (with doves and pigeons as an option for the poor), flour and oil and some elaborate blood-letting. Only then could the person be allowed back in the city and resume their place in the community.

I realise this is an extensive preamble to the leprosy healing miracles of Jesus. It is not given as an attempt to make the process of reader-response criticism another academic discipline. It is, however, an illustration of what is available in the text itself in order to use the knowledge it contains to inform the imagination we seek to bring. I have only used a readily available word search program and quoted from one dictionary article in describing the biblical setting for the miracles we are studying in this chapter. [31] The detail is all contained in the Bible and just needs a little investigation in order to set the miracle in context. By putting greater emphasis on the scriptural resource available in this chapter, I hope the reader will be more confident in searching for the meaning of the *healing beyond the miracle.*

The healing of one leper is recorded by Mark (1:40-45), Matthew (8:1-4) and Luke (5:12-16). We should recognise that Jesus cleanses

---

[31] In this book I have consistently used two computer programs to support my research. They are Accordance 8.1.3 (*www.accordancebible.com*) and Libronix Digital Library System 1.2.2 (203) (*www.libronix.com*)

the leper, which is considered a healing, but none of the words for healing are used in this passage. The healing concentrates on making the person clean so that he can be reinstated as a member of his community. In addition to the cure of the disease there would be a healing of social relationships. This man is breaking the rules though when he comes to Jesus. He does not call out to warn him of his disease, and in Luke's version he even comes into the city. Mark reports that Jesus was moved with pity or compassion, although there are some manuscripts that suggest this phrase should read, "...moved with anger." [32] Regardless of Jesus' emotion, all three versions have the leper saying the same thing: "Lord[33], if you choose, you can make me clean."

We have already discovered that leprosy was largely thought of as an incurable disease, but we have no indication from the context of the Gospel writers why the man thought it was possible. It is the first miracle where Jesus is moved with compassion; it is the first healing recorded in Matthew's account and follows on from the theme of the Great Sermon, suggesting it is the first person he encounters as he descends the mountain; it is an early recorded healing in Luke similar to the ordering in Mark. There is nothing in the context to suggest that the man should expect healing, but he dares to present himself in the manner he does.

Like the woman with an issue of blood – another person in a state of uncleanliness but more bold – he seeks healing from Jesus. Unlike the woman he does not rob Jesus of power; he asks for compassion/pity. Jesus responds by stretching out his hand and touching the leper, saying to him, "I do choose. Be made clean." Unusually all three writers exactly record this progression. It must tell us something about the accuracy of this recollection that all three mirror the response. All agree that he was immediately cleansed and that the leper was to show himself to the priest saying nothing to anyone. We do not know what happens next, but the result is that Jesus is unable to operate without a large crowd surrounding him wherever he goes.

---

[32] A fuller reflection is given in Hooker, Morna D. *Black's New Testament Commentaries: The Gospel According to St Mark.* London: A & C Black, 1991. p79/80

[33] Not in Mark

The other story about the cleansing of leprosy involves the ten lepers living in the region between Samaria and Galilee. It is one of the last healing miracles recorded by Luke and happens on the way to Jesus' triumphal entry into Jerusalem (17:11-19). Luke alone records this miracle, and there are no parallels in the other Gospels. The content and the detail of the story mark it as being different from the healing previously recorded by him. It is speculative to reason why Luke alone records this story, but perhaps the other writers were intent on telling the story of Jesus' passion and the events leading up to the cross, given the proximity of that event. Unlike in the previous story, the lepers call out to Jesus. On this occasion they ask Jesus to have mercy on them. His response is to tell them to go to the priest so that the cleansing could be verified within the Laws of Moses.

The leper that returned was a Samaritan. This is significant because it is the only healing that specifically involves a Samaritan. [34] The other thing that it highlights is the difference between healing and salvation in Luke's telling of this story. All ten were cleansed as in the previous story, but the one who returned to give thanks was additional saved as a result of his thanksgiving. The distinction is made in the use of a Greek word rarely used in the healing miracles: *sozein* ('to save', indicating complete healing or wholeness, being at one with God.)

There is reference to Simon the Leper in scripture (Mark 14:3-9, Matthew 26:6-13), but it is unclear whether this was someone cured of the disease, a nickname given to the person to differentiate him from others, or a coded reference to another character named elsewhere in the text. Others have posited suggestions, but none of the theories affect the direction of our thinking at this point as we return to our quest to find the *healing beyond the miracle.* I want to tell the above story again but from the diary entry of Aaron Kohen, the priest in charge of the synagogue the day eleven people with leprosy presented themselves for the ceremony of ritual cleaning, and his reflection on the events that had taken place.

This was a day like none before, and I suspect I will never see anything like it again. You might say that "a funny thing

---

[34] There is a helpful article on Wikipedia that explains the significance and importance of this point. Follow the link: *en.wikipedia.org/wiki/Samaritan*

happened on the way to the synagogue today," and you would be right. I was passing by the city rubbish dump when a voice called out, "Rabbi Kohen." It was Simon the Leper, breathless and excited, running toward me.

I told him to stop and reminded him that he was not allowed anywhere near the city gates. He refused to go back and asked me to look at him claiming that he had no red, yellow or white spots anyway. He insisted that I needed to give him a check up and to start the ceremony. He even had two birds ready for the service.

I agreed to look, and sure enough there was no sign of the disease; his skin was soft and pure without blemish or scar. It was amazing. In all my years as a priest I have never known of anyone getting cured of a skin complaint. I asked him what had happened, and he explained that he took a chance and fell at the feet of Jesus as he was passing by. At first he thought he was angry that he had broken the rules and gone to him without giving him the required warning. Simon went on to explain that, far from being annoyed, Jesus was full of compassion and stretched out his hand to touch him. I still cannot quite believe it. As far as I was aware only Naaman and Miriam have ever been cured of leprosy and both of these were in exceptional circumstances. Surely Jesus is not in the same league as Moses and Elisha?

Simon explained that he would have come earlier but had stopped to celebrate his good fortune and tell everyone that would listen about what Jesus had done. I had heard my colleague down the road in Capernaum say that Jesus had healed many people the previous day outside the fisherman's house. I had to look at the Torah to see what I needed to do next, and later in the day while I was preparing the wood, yarn and hyssop I heard shouting outside.

As I looked out I could see another nine people from the nearby leper colony asking me to come to them. This was turning out to be a very unusual day indeed. They said they were cured and had each brought two birds to start the ceremony. Was this a joke that another Rabbi was playing on me? I examined each in turn and they were all spotless. I now had twenty birds and all the paraphernalia needed to do the first part of the ceremony, and after so long being away from their loved ones, they all wanted *the service done there and then. They all had to wash their clothes, have a shave and take a bath. I wondered where I was going to get ten tents for the week...*

Then, just as I thought I had everything organised, another person requested I inspect their sudden healing. From never having anyone cured from the illness, I now had eleven people seeking ceremonial cleansing after the skin diseases had disappeared. At least the last person was very grateful for my help and extremely polite. He described the moment when Jesus had told him to go and show himself to the priest and how his skin had repaired before his very eyes. I asked why he had not returned with the others, and he explained that he had gone back to Jesus to say thank you. Seemed obvious, I suppose, that you would want to do that, and I wondered why the others had not. Then he said that Jesus had responded to his thanksgiving by saying, "Get up and go on your way; your faith has made you well." But this was a Samaritan!

Anyway I eventually got them all sorted. The birds were sacrificed and the blood used to sprinkle blessing on each one of them seven times. They had all completed their ablutions and settled down in their tents inside the city, and as I returned home I thought about all the things that would be required in seven days' time.

As I lay down I began to ponder on what Jesus had done. My role was to make the lepers outcast and separate them from the community that wanted to support them. He touched the untouchable, and instead of excluding them he made them feel included. The law would bind the lepers to the places outside the city, whereas Jesus had unbound them and welcomed them into the community. The law was designed to make sure that the community was ordered and organized, but were the rules right? Should the law condemn some to a life separated from the rest of us? Jesus seemed to be healing body, mind, emotions, faith and relationships by his compassion and courage; what did the synagogue do other than discipline, chastise and criticise? After all, the illness is only skin deep and the person remains. I was left to ponder all these things, but it would not be the last challenge that Jesus was to make and one day I would have to answer the questions I posed myself.

I think that the priests must, at least, have questioned their own belief structure as a result of the lepers presenting themselves following the cleansing they received. Eight days later the community to which they returned must have been challenged by the miracle of which the lepers had been a part. With the Torah (law) being so integral to the faith of the nation, how could the healing of an incurable disease not have an effect on the people who saw the miracle take place? Would it have brought to mind the story of Moses and Miriam, or more likely, the healing of the Syrian commander Naaman who was asked to wash himself seven times in the River Jordan? These were momentous stories of the faith that affected countless others. Surely, the actions of Jesus had an impact on people other than those who directly benefitted. But what was it? Were people more disposed to look out for each other, care for each other, have compassion for each other, include and not exclude, share bread and fellowship one with another? Were they seeing the value of community living rather than individual living?

And by the way – does any of this say anything to us today?

CHAPTER SIX

You've got to Hand it to Him

It is many years since Sunday was considered by some a day of rest. In the UK, the *Keep Sunday Special* campaign was started as a Christian letter-writing pressure group urging the government not to allow further opportunity for Sunday Trading. Since that debate was lost and the Sunday Trading Bill (1996) was passed, the group have sought to limit further erosion of Sunday as a significant non-working day. Their website says:

> *We believe in having time for family, friends and community. We believe in time to rest and enjoy ourselves. We believe in working hard and living life to the full. And we believe in keeping just one day a week a bit special. "* [35]

The five reasons they give for keeping Sunday special are:

- Protecting Relationships
- Preserving Community
- Saving Local Business
- Respecting Faith
- Getting Rest

I was interested to learn more about the faith aspect of the movement's view. It simply said:

> *For many people in this country, Sunday has a particular religious significance as a day set aside for worship and a day*

---

[35] *www.keepsundayspecial.org.uk/Web/Content/Default.aspx?Content=87* (accessed 01.07.11)

that's different from the rest of the week. Of course it's a view that's not shared by everyone in our multicultural Britain, but it's a view that we should respect.

This suggests that the major reason for keeping Sunday special is no longer on religious grounds as once it might have been. In Islamic countries some shops are closed on Fridays during midday prayers and in Israel many shops are closed on Friday evening and Saturday during daytime. The Christian emphasis of keeping Sabbath seems to have almost disappeared!

The next healing miracle to consider takes place on the Sabbath. It would help if we were able to understand why the timing is so significant in the story of the man with a withered hand who was healed by Jesus in the synagogue (Mark 3:1-6, Matthew 12:9-14 and Luke 6:6-11). The term 'Sabbath' derives from the Hebrew *Shabbat* (שַׁבָּת), 'to cease', which was first used in the biblical account for the seventh day of creation (Genesis 2:2-3). The fact that the Creator rested on the seventh day after six days of cosmic toil became one of the covenant imperatives for the people of God. It is contained in the Ten Commandments (Exodus 20, Deuteronomy 5), emphasizing that the Lord had blessed and consecrated the day. Deuteronomy explains:

> **Deuteronomy 5:14-15**
> *The seventh day is a Sabbath to the Lord your God; you shall not do any work—you, or your son or your daughter, or your male or female slave, or your ox or your donkey, or any of your livestock, or the resident alien in your towns, so that your male and female slave may rest as well as you. Remember that you were a slave in the land of Egypt and the Lord your God brought you out from there with a mighty hand and an outstretched arm; therefore the Lord your God commanded you to keep the Sabbath day.*

There is a sense of justice for all in this command as it relates not only to the people of Israel but to everyone who is part of the household whether they believe or not. The reverence for Sabbath is best summarized by the conversation recorded in Exodus between Moses and God:

> **Exodus 31:12-17**
> *The LORD said to Moses: You yourself are to speak to the Israelites: "You shall keep my Sabbaths, for this is a sign*

between me and you throughout your generations, given in order that you may know that I, the LORD, sanctify you. You shall keep the Sabbath, because it is holy for you; everyone who profanes it shall be put to death; whoever does any work on it shall be cut off from among the people. Six days shall work be done, but the seventh day is a Sabbath of solemn rest, holy to the LORD; whoever does any work on the Sabbath day shall be put to death. Therefore the Israelites shall keep the Sabbath, observing the Sabbath throughout their generations, as a perpetual covenant. It is a sign forever between me and the people of Israel that in six days the LORD made heaven and earth and on the seventh day he rested and was refreshed.

This stress upon permanency and partnership adds strength to the commandment, and the punishment for non-compliance is immediate and uncompromising. In later writings, the prophet Isaiah extends the covenant made with God to any who keep the Sabbath (Isaiah 56), and Jeremiah asserts that those who hallow the Sabbath and do not take burdens out of their homes and to the Temple will be blessed; although the prophet notes that the people had "stiffened their necks and would not hear or receive instruction"(Jeremiah 17:23). By the time of the second Temple, Nehemiah introduced Sabbath reforms, seeing the people disregarding the former laws and working. He locked the gates of Jerusalem on the Friday night and prevented the merchants from trading. He even threatened to "lay hands on them" (Nehemiah 13:21) if they persisted in camping outside the walls of the City on Friday evenings.

There is not space in this work to deal fully with the transition from first to second Temple attitudes, faith, culture and ordinance, but it is necessary to indicate that the changes were significant to the identity of the Jews. The proud and successful tribes that were under the leadership of the godly, appointed King David had conquered their neighbours and established themselves as a prominent nation. They had had a successful warrior king, the architect's drawings of a great Temple, a growing prosperity through trade and commerce and a distinct cultic monotheistic faith in Yahweh to influence and encourage them. It did not last; first the Assyrian army invaded the northern kingdom, shortly followed by Babylonian aggression in the south. The Temple was destroyed and the people scattered. The leadership in exile was left to consider why God had allowed these things to happen, and when they eventually returned they concluded that their disobedience was to blame and they must return to the original covenantal relationship that they had once enjoyed with God. This is why the priests put greater emphasis in cultic observance to the laws established by Moses.

To ensure the people knew exactly what was required of them, rabbinic scholars discussed the extent of the law's purpose and meaning at length. The result was an enlarged version of the Torah with Midrash and Talmudic explanations ensuring the people lived under the authority of God and His commandment as understood by the Pharisees. An example of this is the thirty-nine *melakhot* describing the categories of activities that were (are) deemed work. The list includes carrying, burning, extinguishing, finishing, writing, erasing, cooking, washing, sewing, tearing, knotting, untying, shaping, ploughing, planting, reaping, harvesting, threshing, winnowing, selecting, sifting, grinding, kneading, combing, spinning, dyeing, chain-stitching, warping, weaving, unravelling, building, demolishing, trapping, shearing, slaughtering, skinning, tanning, smoothing and marking. It is important to understand that these are general categories. In a modern example for instance, mowing the lawn would fit into a few categories, including ploughing, reaping and harvesting. [36]

Let us return to the healing miracle of Jesus that took place in a synagogue on the Sabbath, involving a man with a withered hand. This is one of four healings that take place in a synagogue and one of seven that take place on the Sabbath. It is the only recording throughout the Bible of Jesus being angry (Mark 3:5) and is the miracle that led to the first plot to kill Jesus (Matthew 12:14).

Jesus challenges the legalism that places higher value on a sheep than a man. He has already asserted that the Sabbath was made for man, not man for the Sabbath (Mark 2:27) and asks the Pharisee the question, "Which is lawful on the Sabbath: to do good or to do evil, to save life or to destroy it?"

---

[36] A helpful website for further investigation of this subject is: *www.ou.org/chagim/shabbat/concept.htm* (accessed 05.07.11)

The man whose right [37] hand was withered was attending the synagogue and appears to be there for worship and learning only. There is no indication in the text that he was specifically there for healing or to meet Jesus. He is simply 'there' and is used by Jesus to be the physical illustration of a point – a point that he makes earlier in the context of all three Gospels in explaining how he is the Lord of the Sabbath. In each of the accounts the healing miracle is preceded by the controversy involving the disciples picking at the corn on a previous Sabbath. Given the temple view of Sabbath work prohibition and the *melakhot* above, a quick glance suggests Jesus and his disciples are guilty of reaping, harvesting, threshing, winnowing, grinding, to name but a few. They were probably also guilty of travelling beyond a Sabbath's day's journey of around 2000 cubits, or ½ mile (Exodus 16:29, Numbers 35:5, Josiah 3:4).

It is no wonder that the law-abiding Pharisee do not know how to understand these actions. Then 'to add insult to injury', the perpetrator of the crime, Jesus, turns around and gets angry with them! It is not our place to defend the actions of the Pharisees, but the reader might have some sympathy faced by such a challenge. The law prohibits the action but Jesus' reasoned argument is persuasive. The dilemma is to agree with Jesus and jettison the law that has restored order in society or to dispose of the person causing the problem. We know the result of course, and the final verse in each of the Gospel writer's telling of the story speaks of conspiracy, fury and destructive intent. But what of the man who was healed, and can we imagine any *healing beyond the miracle?*

In the following short story, *The Case of the Withered Hand*, we join the investigation of Shylock Homes as he delves into the effects of an extraordinary event in the synagogue two weeks previous. He has been commissioned by the Pharisees and Herodians to gather the necessary evidence in order to convict Jesus, the miracle worker. He has been paid a large advance and told to dig up everything he can to make sure the conviction is watertight. But the detective does not anticipate so many people being so defensive of the man.

---

[37] According to Gospel-writer Luke

Case opened 20 April Year 30

I always knew this was going to be a strange case when the Pharisaic and Herodian parties approached me together. They rarely speak with each other so when they each paid large advances to secure a conviction my antennae were twitching. Apparently a man called Jesus had gone into the synagogue and told Mr. William Withers to stretch out his shrivelled hand at the beginning of morning worship on the Sabbath. This had resulted in his limb being restored. It was my job to get enough eyewitness statements in order to have Jesus punished by death for working on the Sabbath. The case looked open and shut. It started well with the affidavit signed by the synagogue leader who confirmed everything had happened as the prosecutors had said. But then I went to see Mrs. Marcia Withers who started me thinking this case was not as clear-cut as people were saying.

She explained that Bill had not had a perfect day since a stroke had robbed him of the use of his right hand several years previous. He was by trade a lyre player in the synagogue and local inns – a very good one, she added. Despite not being able to play anymore he was loyal to the synagogue and went there every Sabbath. She recalled the day he went out to worship as usual but returned jumping up and down and excitedly talking of the man who healed his hand. He was stretching it out and spinning it around on its wrist joint with such ferocity that she had cautioned him, "It might fall off if you're not careful!" Mrs. Withers then explained what life had been like for the family since her husband had been taken ill and how she had taken in washing and held down three cleaning jobs as well as having coped with Bill's moods – trying to make the little they had meet the costs of keeping everyone alive.

It wasn't just his hand that had been affected, she explained, but his mind, mood and spirit had also been depressed by his lack of movement. The Synagogue had been useless and had never helped them, she said. Mrs. Withers painted a very graphic picture of hopelessness. I asked her what the future holds. A big smile stretched across her face, and she looked ten years younger as worry-creases fell from her appearance. She exclaimed that Bill was now playing the lyre again and had bookings coming in from all over the region. Not only did they want him to play the musical instrument but also to tell the people about the healing that restored his hope. Bill had become a new man, even better than the one before the stroke. He had a new zest for life and his story was contagious and uplifting, she concluded.

As I left Mrs. Withers I thought about the husband she had gained as a result of the miracle that brought about his cure and saw how much it meant to his wife. Was it so bad that this took place on the Sabbath? I went to see a sheep farmer who had been in the congregation when the incident took place and asked him about the conversation that took place between Jesus and the Synagogue officials. "Pickuach nefesh" he said. I asked him to explain what this meant and he described the circumstances under which life can be saved on the Sabbath. I was surprised that he was able to recite so many examples when the Talmud and Mishna permitted a person to work or perform an action despite the limitations of the Sabbath.

Jesus had got it wrong, according to the sheep farmer, when he had said that a sheep could be lifted out of a pit on the Sabbath. According to him, the best you can do is leave it some feed and go back the next day to lift it out. It is not permitted to save the life of a sheep on the Sabbath. He then confided that he thought the law was an ass, and did those Pharisee know the cost of a sheep these days? In his view the whole Sabbath legislation needed an overhaul, and perhaps Bill's healing might bring this about. The farmer thought that Jesus was very brave – or stupid – to challenge the scribes by getting angry and asking them awkward questions. He had heard that this was not the first time Jesus had tested the Pharisees over the Sabbath laws, and his disciples had goaded them by picking ears of corn and eating the grain. I asked him what he thought about Bill's healing. The farmer was delighted for him and was looking forward to him playing the lyre again in the synagogue. Was he concerned about when and where Jesus carried out the healing, I asked. "By no means," he replied and he hoped that this would result in the laws being revised to enable reasonable work to be done on the Sabbath.

Here was another person who supported the action of Jesus and saw nothing wrong with curing Bill's hand. Yes, Jesus was working outside the law and asserting his power and authority over the temple officials, but was it wrong?

My next witness was an apprentice scribe called Ezra who was studying for a career as a scripture copyist and lawmaker. Surely he would be able to give me the statement that would condemn Jesus. We met in his dingy little room and we went over the events that took place in the Synagogue. It was true that Jesus had broken the letter of the law, he said, but not the spirit of the law. He then spoke at length about the history and development of the Sabbath as instituted by Moses to ensure the people kept focus on YHWH; of course he wouldn't say the name. Jesus was right that it is lawful to do good and not harm, save life rather than destroy it. In Ezra's mind Jesus was fully focused on YHWH and could not be found guilty of breaking the law. He reasoned that only someone of God could heal by command and save life. He had thought about the last part of this – saving life – and had concluded that Jesus must be the Messiah. I asked him if he knew what this meant for him, and he agreed that he could no longer remain part of the Temple authority system and would be seeking a new direction. In fact he was seriously considering being a follower of Jesus! It amazed me that a trainee scribe was convinced that Jesus was right in his actions and left me to ponder my next witness statement.

The last witness I met was Bill's friend who was with him when the healing occurred. This friend, also a musician, played percussion alongside Bill's lyre. They had performed many times together, and when Bill had had his stroke Grover's career in the music business had also been curtailed. He explained that "the sunshine went the day Bill lost his playing hand" but that he had assured him that there would always be the two of them and that he could lean on him and use him. Good to his word, Grover had supported Bill and his wife, Marcia, as best he could. He had prayed that Bill would once again enjoy a lovely day as he had done long before. Grover explained that when Jesus had walked into the Synagogue with a few others nobody had taken much notice. He was a new person to the congregation but his appearance was nothing special and he had given no impression of being especially different. In fact Grover thought he was somewhat ordinary. There had been a commotion, he recalled, followed by a request for Bill to come forward and stand before Jesus. Everything had gone quiet – silent in fact – and Jesus had told Bill to stretch out his hand. Immediately his hand had been restored.

> *I concluded that I must return my fee as I was unable to get the evidence my clients wanted in order to secure a conviction and that Jesus was innocent.*

In telling this story I hope the reader is beginning to understand that each of Jesus' miracles had and has a huge effect upon many more people than those who were cured and healed of the presenting illness. Many of us have breathed a sigh of relief when we learn that someone close to us has come through a period of ill health. A friend and colleague was admitted into hospital with acute pancreatitis that resulted in a year of treatment including life support and intensive nursing. His continuing recovery towards full health has taken a weight off many who feared for his life and had concern for his future. I would argue that few people have an illness that does not affect more than just the person who is suffering, and that it why I believe that there is *healing beyond the miracle.*

CHAPTER SEVEN

There's No Healing Beyond?

Once upon a time, as all good stories begin, in a far off place, there lived a wild man who ran around his shelter in the graveyard with nothing on but a smile, which would stretch from ear to ear every time someone came close to his home among the tombs. He had not always been like this, and as a young boy he had been thought odd but had been popular among the townsfolk.

He ran errands for his seniors and got them their daily fresh fish from the harbour as the boats came in from a night of trawling. He would make believe that he was a seafaring pirate and tell the captain to hand over their catch or be made to walk the plank. He even dressed up for the occasion and donned hat and scarf, breeches and earring. Going by the name of 'jolly jack tar', he would imagine many adventures down by the quayside. There was a hint that something may not be quite right when he was still playing the game at the age of eighteen.

His love of dressing up came at a much earlier age; in fact he was putting on his mother's shoes shortly after he could walk. Every day was a dressing-up day, and he would devise complex stories to match the outfit. One day he draped a red shawl over his head and shoulders and took himself to the woods. He was gone so long that his parents began to worry and gathered the villagers together to look for him. He returned covered in animal hair and told them he had fought a wolf and killed it with an axe. He was scolded and sent to bed with no tea that night. On another occasion he dressed up to look like an elf and said that he was going to Never Never Land to find the lost boys. He returned that day covered in mashed potato explaining that he had had a great time getting involved in a food fight. The scolding was worse this time, and again he was sent to bed.

The real problem came when he went up to the hill where the pigs were kept and started to herd them around the field. It is thought that he may have caught an airborne disease that affected his brain because from that moment he became uncontrollably wild, screaming at everyone he met and laughing at their reaction. The parents could no longer lock him in his room and leave him without food. In fact, the town council agreed that he was so antisocial that they put a restraining order on him, banished him from his home and told to live away from everyone. On a number of occasions they tried physically to tether him to a post, but each time he broke free. They tried ropes and cables but nothing could hold him. They even tried to chain him, but again he managed to escape. He spent his days in deep conversation with the pigs high on the hill and would call out in a variety of voices depending on who he thought he was from hour to hour. His clothes had worn out and fell from his muscular frame giving him the appearance of nudity. Some of the local lads would challenge each other as to how long they could stay in the graveyard or how close they could get to 'Legion' as they nicknamed him. None of them got closer than the first gravestone or lasted more than five minutes; such was the speed and terror of the demoniac.

A couple of the older people in the town who remembered his kindness as a boy left food for him but never ventured very close and were too frightened of him to stop and chat. So his days were spent in solitude and isolation; his mind wandered further and he became confused. On a good day he would sit quietly and sob as he realised that his life was going to be lonely and empty – yes, this was a good day, because most days were manic and frantic as paranoia and schizophrenia controlled his thoughts and movements. By now, he was completely wild and out of control, even of himself. He was surrounded by death, far away from the seashore and was developing an unnatural fear of the swineherd, which had now become his guards and oppressors.

But a change was about to happen....

This day was to be a day that no other day had ever been and a day that no other day could be again. It was the day when the demoniac was born again; by the end of this day he would live in a totally new way free from voices in his head and able to take control of his own life. It started like any other day. He had fitful sleep and had been disturbed by the characters within that were his constant companions. The morning was chilly – not that 'hot' and 'cold' were ever his gauges of temperature. He found some bread left by one of the villagers and picked some sour berries from a thorn bush – not that he could distinguish between sweet and tart. He roared and cowered at the pigs on the hill depending on who was controlling him at the time. He looked at a puddle that had formed after the rain the previous night and convinced himself that he was two people and that both had a multiplicity of characters within.

Then something caught his attention, and he heard the shuffle of feet nearby. He hid behind one of the tombs thinking it was the kids up to their old games. As he jumped out and bellowed his scariest "Boo!" he was surprised to see that it was not the local children but a man with many followers. The demoniac did not know the man, but he addressed him as 'Jesus, Son of the Most High God'. Nobody knows where this sudden recognition had come from or how he identified Jesus, but divine revelation had been given and at that moment the demoniac knew that he could be healed and pleaded with Jesus not to prolong his mental agony. With compassion and concern Jesus asked the man his name, but he could not say as the personalities within began to fight for supremacy. It was clear that the demoniac and the pigs had become entwined in the mind of the man and separation would be difficult. Jesus simply said, "Go!" and the man was cured. At the same time the pigs became manic and charged toward the cliff edge and, without stopping, plummeted to the rocks below.

Those farmers looking after the pigs were naturally disappointed to see their stock commit suicide by going over the edge and decided that the healing was somehow tied in with their loss. They returned to the town and canvassed support from the civic authorities to return to the scene in order to challenge Jesus. As they approached, Jesus and the man – now completely cured of his mental illness – were sitting enjoying the man's first normal conversation. Now I would have expected there to be great rejoicing and thanksgiving for the miracle that had occurred, but the people were more concerned about the herd that was lost.

The fear they had for the demoniac was not totally gone, but they appeared more frightened of Jesus who they believed was even more dangerous. They asked him to leave their region and not return. Jesus got up and the man got up to join him, but Jesus told him to stay and tell his story to anyone who would listen.

At this point the story should finish with the words "and they all lived happily ever after" but it does not because the man went away and did as Jesus instructed. He told his story throughout the ten cities in the area. Some were amazed but most thought of him as a man of fairy tales and fantasy. He did not return home to his village as the people remained uncertain whether the healing was lasting and whether he might return to his former mental state. His parents thought like the rest of his village, and the people in charge of the pigs never let him forget the day that cost them their livelihood. In many ways he remained alone and with a story that unsettled those he met, similar to the reaction he had got among the tombs. As for Jesus, his story continued to challenge and upset some people but was a source of healing and encouragement to others. His story only had a happy ending for those who understood and believed.

I think this is the miracle that has no added healing. It is the exception to the *healing beyond the miracle* as there appears to be nobody in the story that witnessed the event who we can argue received a benefit from the miracle. If we were to take the traditional meaning of the miracle, it is about Gentiles and impurity, with Jesus seen to be crossing the boundaries.

The Decapolis, meaning 'ten cities', is situated in a non-Jewish area southeast of Lake Galilee. The miracle is set among the tombs, a place of impurity, involving a man without clothes, another sign of impurity, in a Gentile area, yet another example of impurity. Jesus chooses to cross the lake and arrives in this area, perhaps blown there by the storm that is recorded by all three Gospel writers immediately prior to the miracle. Was it chance that caused him to take his first visit to a Gentile area? Providentially, the person that everyone else is afraid of is able to declare the lordship of Jesus and give him a title that even the disciples are yet to discover. Matthew tells the story with two demoniacs again needing to have a witness to the miracle for the purposes of his readership, whereas Mark and Luke repeat the story with only minor variations.

Returning to the geographical setting challenges our view of another miracle that we will consider later involving the Syrophoenician woman. Many argue that Jesus is somehow convicted by the woman to serve Jew and Gentile alike and that this encounter is the first occasion when Jesus heals a non-Jew. Clearly the miracle of the man with the pigs (often referred to as the Gerasene demoniac) seems to counter this claim – unless we believe that the man was a Jew and had been exiled to the area. This illustrates one of the weaknesses of reader-response criticism because it allows interpretations that may be disconnected from a larger narrative that could inform and enrich the text. For instance, there is reference in Isaiah 65:4 to those "who sit among the graves and spend their nights keeping secret vigil; who eat the flesh of pigs..." It is a prophetic word of judgment and salvation and concludes with a proclamation that God will create a new heaven and a new earth where never again will infant die before they have lived a full life, people are rewarded for their endeavours, God will hear their prayers and "the wolf and the lamb will feed together" (Isaiah 65:17-25). We are aware from Acts 8:30 that the book of Isaiah was published and read, as it appears in the story of Philip and the Ethiopian eunuch. We also know that each of the Gospel writers quote passages from Isaiah, so we can conclude that Jesus was also aware of the prophet's writings. Is it possible that Jesus performs this healing to reference his followers to the vision contained in the prophet writings to which it may allude? The weakness of the approach can, however, be corrected by the reader developing a wider knowledge of biblical context. This should not put the reader off coming to the text with the knowledge they have and searching for the quiet and hidden voices buried in the text. With encouragement and practice the reader is likely to want to delve further into scripture in order to find even more context to the passage they wish to understand. One of the purposes of this book is to empower the reader to look at text with confidence, not relying on the trained theologian, but believing that their view is relevant and appropriate. If that releases and liberates people to want to mine the scriptures for further hidden gems and treasures then this work has achieved its task.

Returning to the miracle we have considered above, I repeat my belief that this miracle had no other healing of a witness or bystander that I could imagine. We could argue that the disciples received healing of their misunderstanding (on this occasion about the divinity of Jesus) but theirs is an audible voice in text and we are looking for the hidden. I am content with my own inability to seek out the hidden in this story and welcome the readers to find it for themselves. It does however raise a question for me about the seeming 'randomness' of Jesus' healing miracles. Who are the miracles for? Why are some healed and not others? How is the choice made? John refers to the miracles as signs and indicates that many more were done than those recorded (John 20:30).

Thinking about signs for a moment and considering the meaning of the word, we soon find that there are many interpretations. A sign can be an indicator, a mark, a gesture or motion, a notice, a trace, a symbol, a language, a warning or omen, or a signature, to name but a few meanings. On a journey, signs are used to help the traveller to the destination, highlighting hazards along the way and warning them of the local laws and bylaws. As the traveller we can choose to accept the signs and adhere to the instructions they offer or ignore them and find our own way. A friend of mine will never continue along a signposted route if it means queuing in traffic. I am unconvinced that it saves time, but he does get to the destination via his sometimes-circuitous route. I do think he uses more energy in his decision to keep moving regardless of the conditions. We often refer to our faith as a journey, and the miracles are sign(post)s for us to choose to follow. Each of them has something to inform or stimulate our thinking, and study of them will rarely leave us untouched by the message that God is conveying to us.

Far from being 'random', the healing miracles help to build a picture of the desire of God's heart for everyone, both at the time when Jesus performed them and by the power of the Holy Spirit today. Jesus gave a sign to those who chose to understand it then, and that same sign is available to those that choose to understand now.

Healing and deliverance ministry is a response to Jesus' command to his disciples, giving them authority to drive out evil spirits and to heal every disease and sickness (Matthew 10:1). Interestingly the Great Commission commands followers to "go and make disciples of

84

all nations, baptising them ... and teaching them" (Matthew 28:19-20). Great care must be taken to understand each miracle in its own context so that miracles are not used as a commodity in our age that can be bottled up and sold. Such devaluation and commercialism cannot be found in Jesus' action then and should not be encouraged now. Jesus asked for nothing more than acceptance and belief. Healing for sale should be avoided at any and all costs. Harold Willmington of Liberty University suggests an eight-fold purpose for Jesus' miracles [38] (not healing miracles alone) as follows:

1. Matthew 8:16-17 — To fulfil Old Testament Prophecy
2. John 3:1-2 — To validate His message
3. John 2:11a — To reveal His glory
4. John 2:11b — To increase the faith of His disciples
5. John 6:14 — To declare His messianic claims
6. Matthew 14:32-33 — To prove His deity
7. Matthew 20:34 et al. — To demonstrate His compassion
8. Luke 5:20-24 — To show His authority to forgive sin

The healing of the Gerasene demoniac fulfils each of the purposes described by Willmington. The Old Testament prophecy may not be fulfilled, but Jesus certainly had it in mind as he drove out the demons and healed the man of his mental illness. In so doing he confirmed his message that he came to save the world and not to condemn it. The demoniac calls out a title that declares him as Jesus, son of the Most High God, and the healing reveal his glory, affirms his deity and supports his messianic claims. In the touching conclusion to the healing the two men sit talking, and I am sure they would be words of comfort, support and encouragement. The Lucan version of the story uses the Greek word *sozein* to describe the healing that took place, and we have discussed the significance of this complete, wholesome version of healing in Chapter Three.

In trying to get to the *healing beyond the miracle*, we are attempting to reach the people that benefitted, were influenced and/or were affected by the miracle in positive ways. The townsfolk were

---

[38] Harold Willmington, *What you need to know about Jesus' Miracles: Healing* digitalcommons.liberty.edu/cgi/viewcontent.cgi?article=1031&context=wil l_know accessed 010310

clearly unwilling to have Jesus stay and appeared more fearful of him than of the demoniac. At least, they never asked the demoniac to leave the region. There does not appear to be any supporter as in the case of the paralytic and many other healing miracle stories. There is no community in support, and unlike in the case of the lepers, there is no cultic reparation ceremony that reinstates the healed man. There is no one urging Jesus to heal the man as Jairus and others did for their relative or friend, and there is no crowd to witness the healing. It is left to the man now restored to proclaim the actions of Jesus to any who might listen. This may be one of the few places where the efficacy of the miracle might be found, and if the reader wants to find a voice this could be the best place to look and imagine.

We travel from the shores of Gennesaret to arrive at the setting of our next miracle. We will have no difficulty in establishing a third party recipient of healing in our next story.

CHAPTER EIGHT

Crumbs, Even the Dogs Get Better

There can be no *healing beyond the miracle* for people outside the Jewish faith if Jesus only came to minister to his own. This is the issue addressed by our next miracle of the healing of a Syrophoenician/Canaanite daughter (Mark 7:24-31, Matthew 15:21-28). Is this Jewish chauvinism or a message that Jesus wishes to share in an unorthodox manner that borders on offensive? There are certain similarities in this story with the healing of the centurion's servant (Matthew 8:5-13, Luke 7:1-10) and the healing of the Royal Official's son (John 4:46-54). Later, we will try to imagine a story that weaves these three healings together. All three miracles are performed at a distance, with the sufferer 'back home', by a word from Jesus as a result of a loved one's faith. Jesus' mission was to the people of Israel, so what made Jesus react to the request of an outsider? Hooker suggests:

> *His [Jesus'] healing miracles are closely linked with his preaching: they are part of the breaking-in of God's Kingdom. Jesus calls Israel to repent and believe the gospel and Israel's response is a mixture of enthusiasm and incomprehension, belief and rejection; the healing miracles are closely tied up with his proclamation and take place only where there is faith. The Gentile woman requests a cure outside the context of Jesus' call to Israel; she seems to be asking for a cure that is detached from the in breaking of God's Kingdom, merely taking advantage of the opportunity provided by the presence of a miracle worker. This is perhaps the reason for Jesus' stern answer; his healings are part of something greater and cannot be torn out of context.*

> *Mark does not interpret the woman's reply as simply a witty retort; by accepting Jesus' terms, she recognizes that salvation belongs to Israel and shows her faith in something more far reaching than a miraculous power to heal.* [39]

The three healings together provide reassurance to the Gentile hearers of the Gospels that Jesus is prepared and ready to give them a share in the blessings of the Kingdom. Jesus has already shown his willingness to speak to women despite the cultural taboo, and like the woman at the well this is a woman outside the people of Israel. Then it was a Samaritan; now it is a woman originally from Phoenicia in Syria. The area is a little north of Galilee and is likely to have been multi-ethnic with Jew and Gentile sharing the space and the trade that took place there. Matthew describes the ethnicity of the woman as Canaanite, probably to emphasize to his Jewish readership that this woman was Gentile. He also inserts a plea from the disciples to send her away because she kept shouting at them. As we have indicated before, Matthew is keen in his writing to ensure that the reader/hearer knows that the incident can be validated by eyewitnesses. Mark inserts his familiar tone of secrecy saying that Jesus had entered a house and did not want anyone to know he was there. In these two variants we can glimpse at the tools and devices used by the writer to get to his implied or intended reader. The modern reader will not have been considered when the author put the story together, so we bring other understanding to the text which enables us to find additional meaning, not necessarily intended but still valid.

Jesus' use of the word 'dog' has puzzled readers throughout the ages, and many have tried to soften the impact by speculating that the Syrophoenician woman was included in a wider reference. It was probably as offensive to her as are many modern idioms today that polarize sections of our communities. But that which she needed from Jesus made it worth enduring the insult. The text provides a complex exchange in the movement and direction of the conversation, and we cannot tell what the body language was saying. That is left to our imagination and the attitudes and character we bring to the story. My

---

[39] Morna D. Hooker. *The Gospel According to St Mark*. A & C Black (Publishers) Limited 1991 p182

nuancing of the dialogue is very likely to be very different from yours. However, the result is achieved and the woman is told that the demon has left her daughter. Her great faith made her believe that even a crumb that fell from the table could be of benefit to her. She would of course not know whether Jesus had healed her daughter until she got home; when she did the girl was lying on the bed. I wonder what the babysitter thought when the girl was healed, and did it happen quietly or was the mother told of a dramatic event that gave evidence of the cure? The subject of this miracle and the two others that we consider below are remarkably missing from the stories. We learn little or nothing about them and, in common with others, we learn nothing about the longer-term effects.

The next miracle we consider is John's account of the healing of the Royal Official's son in Cana. This is the second sign in the Gospel, the first occurring in the same place where Jesus turned water into wine at a wedding (John 2:1-11). The actual healing takes place fifteen miles away in Capernaum where the son of a Royal Official lies gravely ill. John sets up this story by reiterating a point he makes in his prologue that, "He came to that which was his own, but his own would not receive him." (John 1:11) Before he re-enters Cana he travels from Samaria and has his encounter with the woman at the well, where the villagers affirm him as Saviour of the world (John 4:42) But the aside that "a prophet has no honour in his own country" (John 4:44) indicates the challenge Jesus faces in getting his own people to accept him as from God. Enter then the Royal Official, a servant of King Herod who has power, authority and status but is helpless in keeping his son alive unless he is able to successfully plead his case with Jesus. This is the first healing miracle recorded by John, and DeCenso believes it is the very first healing miracle that Jesus performs (see Appendix two).

What inspired the official to believe that a Jewish teacher would respond to his request? Where did his confidence come from to believe that Jesus could heal his son? We often approach the text with simple acceptance without asking some obvious questions. Did the official have divine insight, or were his desperate actions the work of a father who, by dint of his status, could command audience with anyone? How did the man feel when Jesus rebuked him by saying, "Unless you see signs and wonders you will not believe"? His recorded polite response was to request that Jesus would come down before his little son dies. What then were his inner feelings when dismissed by Jesus albeit with an assurance that his son would live?

The conclusion of the story is known before it is recorded by John, and understandably it suggests that the official simply believes and starts on his way home. There are no emotions described, and it is left to the reader to imagine the scene. As a dad with a son I will bring the emotions I would feel to this story: it makes the official angry and uneasy to be dismissed without knowing whether he is being brushed-away or healing really has occurred. There is a sense of this relief when the slaves meet him to say that the son lives. It becomes important to know the timing of the healing to ensure that it was of Jesus and not just a coincidence. Only when it is proven that the times are the same does the man truly believe. As a result his whole household believes. I hope the slaves became servants and he considers continued employment with King Herod very carefully. There is clearly *healing beyond the miracle* in this example, but the voices of the womenfolk and the staff are largely silent and we are given the briefest insight of the father. It will only be the reader that can extend this story to make it say the extra that is hidden.

Our third miracle in this chapter involves a centurion and his servant/slave in Capernaum where a number of other miracles take place. Luke tells the story without need for the centurion and Jesus to ever meet. In Luke's account the centurion first of all sends the Jewish elders to get Jesus to come to his home where a highly valued slave is ill and close to death. We learn that he loves the Jewish people and has built them a synagogue. Jesus accedes to their request and journeys toward the house but before the two meet, the centurion sends friends to say, "Do not come further," and "Just speak the word so that the servant is healed." He reasons that as a leader with soldiers under him he gives an order and it is obeyed, so Jesus saying the word will have similar affect. Jesus responds, "I tell you, not even in Israel have I found such faith." Without seeing or meeting Jesus, Luke reports this miracle as a distant healing via Jewish intermediaries. Matthew tells the story very differently. The centurion comes to Jesus as he enters Capernaum and appeals on behalf of his servant who is lying at home paralyzed, in great distress. Jesus offers to come home with the centurion, at which point the versions converge and he asks Jesus to simply "speak the word." The recorded response is longer in Matthew's account:

Matthew 8:11-12

Truly I tell you, in no one in Israel have I found such faith. I tell you, many will come from east and west and will eat with Abraham and Isaac and Jacob in the kingdom of heaven, while the heirs of the kingdom will be thrown into the darkness, where there will be weeping and gnashing of teeth.

The result is the same and the servant is healed.

They are clearly the same story and different from John's episode above. Why are they told so differently? Morris believes that Matthew, as he often does, abbreviates the story and leaves out what he considers inessential detail. "What a man does through agents he does, it may be said, himself." He continues:

So Matthew simply gives the gist of the centurion's communication to Jesus, whereas Luke in greater detail gives the actual sequence of events. Perhaps we can discern something of the differing purposes of the two Evangelists in their treatment of the messengers. Matthew was concerned primarily with the centurion's faith and nationality; to him the messengers were irrelevant, even a distraction. But Luke was interested in the man's character and specifically his humility: to him the messengers were a vital part of the story. [40]

I confess to a little confusion regarding the different accounts of the same story when considering who is *healed beyond the miracle.* Matthew writes to a mainly Jewish audience, and yet in this account Jesus' actions are seen to favour the Gentiles both directly and in consequence. It is a prophetic warning to the Jews and an affront to Jewish exclusivism. Luke on the other hand brings together Jew and Gentile in the story but avoids delivering a prophetic message in favour of a more universal approach. Perhaps this is the point that each writer wants the reader to learn and reinforces the notion of implied, informed and preferred reader. The writer, however, has no choice about the reader; once it leaves their hand the story is at the mercy of those who come to it. Let us try to tell a story that brings

---

[40] Leon Morris. *Luke: An Introduction and Commentary.* Inter-Varsity Press First published 1974 p 151

the three miracles together. Naturally what follows cannot be considered a retelling of the biblical accounts and is merely an attempt to imagine a story from one perspective that suggests a healing that results from the miracles that occur.

I am a slave living by the shoreline just east of a busy port that specialises in exotic trade from countries miles away. I don't know how old I am but I have lived with my present owner for many years. I was born into slavery when my father died at an early age and my mother struggled to feed our family. She took on work with a local merchant while she was pregnant and he didn't have the heart to send her or me away when I was born. The merchant has since died but his wife, a Phoenician woman, carries on the business and she is an excellent mistress. The business is connected to the shipping industry and we make sails for boats of all sizes. It is hard work and long hours but I don't mind because I know that the mistress will look after us. She relies on me and trusts me to get the work done. Recently she put me in charge of the spinnaker area.

There are ten of us slaves and we live in a building next to the big house. Mama is in charge of the living accommodation and she keeps it clean and tidy as best as she is able. She is getting old now, and I sometimes need to help her lift the pan of rice off the stove at meal time. But she still cooks the best John Dory fish in the region and sometimes the mistress will come and join us at mealtime if she gets whiff of the cooking. These are wonderful occasions and we feel like a family. The rest of the slave house is made up of six younger than me from the local areas of Tyre in Canaan and Sidon in Lebanon although both cities are now in Syria, I was told recently. Then there is a man from way down south in Judea from the city of Hebron, a loner from Qumran and a recent acquisition by the mistress from Capernaum. Mama is not a slave; she is a servant because she has worked with the mistress for so long she is free to go. We are all pleased that she doesn't because who would look after us?

The new man from Capernaum, Reuben, is very interesting and tells us all about life round Lake Galilee. I would like to go there one day. He said that I should and he felt sure that I could make sails for the boats there. I won't go, mind, because the mistress is so kind, and I am sure I wouldn't find any as good as her. Reuben has a God called Yahweh, and he tells us about him. He reckons that his God made the world in six days and rested on the seventh which is why he should be allowed to rest on Friday night and Saturday up to sunset. I didn't think the mistress would let him get away with that but she has, and she has given us all the same time off – it's unheard of! Reuben also tells us about Jesus, a man he saw before coming to join us. He says that Jesus is the son of David, son of man and the son of God. "Blimey," I said, "Fancy having three dads! I haven't got one!"

He had to explain further. "He's the son of David because he is the one that the Jews have been waiting for who will defeat the Romans." (I've heard the mistress moaning about the taxes they charge.) "He's the son of man because he has come to save the world." (I'm still unsure what this means and didn't follow what Reuben meant.) "And he is the son of God because he has come directly from heaven to show the world God's love."

I asked Rueben what made him so sure of all this. He explained that he had followed Jesus for a while until his money had run out and had witnessed Jesus doing some amazing things. Apparently, one day a Roman centurion had asked Jesus to make his slave better, and because the soldier had been so convinced that Jesus could do it, the slave got better.

"Wow!" I said, "Do you think he could make me better?" Reuben asked what was wrong with me, and I replied that you could never be too sure and that if this Jesus was about it would not hurt to hedge your bets. More seriously I asked Reuben why a Jewish rabbi would help a non-Jew, and he said that it's what made him so different. We both agreed that he was bound to get into trouble if he carried on helping Gentiles. Especially as Reuben said that it wasn't the only non-Jew he had healed. Apparently one of King Herod's officials, the one that lives in Capernaum, had similarly approached Jesus because his son was ill, and without even visiting the house or touching the little boy, Jesus had made the boy better. I couldn't believe that one – it was too far-fetched – but Rueben swore on his mother's life that it was true (not that he said whether he still had a mother).

It was good that Reuben told me all this because one day the mistress called me up to the house. I was worried that I had done something wrong but didn't know what. When I arrived the mistress was in a very sad and shocked state. Her daughter had picked up a stomach bug from a piece of fish that must have passed its 'best before' date. She said that she had tried all the usual cures, but nothing had worked and the little girl was getting worse. I went through all the therapies we use in the slave house but she had tried them all. Out of desperation I told her about Jesus and asked her to speak to Reuben. He came to the house, and she listened to him tell her about all the signs and wonders he had seen Jesus do. She resolved to travel to Capernaum where Jesus was staying and beg him to heal her little girl. She asked me to stay by her daughter's bedside and keep her cool and hydrated – I had to ask Mama what that meant but between us we did what the mistress asked and she set off.

Hour after hour went by, and the little girl grew weaker and weaker until she was on the point of death. We checked outside; there was no sign of the mistress returning so we went back into the big house and waited. Just as we were about to give up the little girl let out a massive cry, sat up, smiled and asked for a drink and something to eat. The fever had passed and the colour returned to her cheeks. We were delighted and eager to let the mistress know, but it was another day before she returned home. I checked the time when her daughter sat up, and it turned out to be the same time that Jesus had told her to go home following their meeting the day before.

Following the events of that day the mistress released all her slaves from their bonds, but we chose to stay on and we became her servants instead. The work is just as hard, but we are free to go now and she has encouraged us all to believe in Jesus. We went to the synagogue but they were not open to receiving us, so Reuben leads us in prayers and we eagerly await news about Jesus. Some of us hope to see him in Jerusalem at Passover shortly.

CHAPTER NINE

This Needs a Little More

Have you ever met someone who has a faith that could move mountains? As a pastor I am privileged to get alongside people who display strength in circumstances where others might wilt. In a particularly busy period of ministry I was presiding at many funerals and met people at their most vulnerable. The ones that coped best seemed to be the ones that had strong faith. I recall visiting a lady who suffered from a multitude of debilitating conditions and I asked if she would like me to share communion with her. She responded, "My dear boy, I live with Jesus every moment of my day and do not need reminding what he has done for me; he is with me always."

Another old man in a hospice would always get me to open scripture and read aloud so that the rest of the people could hear. He would say that it was impossible to face death unless you were sure that life would continue. As a chaplain of a special needs school where many of the young people had life-limiting diseases, I got a sense of community that is hard to replicate. These children had a good idea of the future and knew roughly the numbers of days they would enjoy in this life and so they did.

Here follow some reports of people who experienced a 'miraculous intervention from God'. [41]

- Woman receives breakthrough after using miracle cloth! – She has been experiencing spiritual attacks but since she attended

---

[41] 'The Miracle Times' is edited by Kyla Cadorin on behalf of The Kingdom Church. Their website is www.bishopclimate.org

deliverance service she has been set free from all the oppression of the enemy.

- Debt cancelled! – For three months she was unable to pay her electricity bill. But God turned it around and froze everything and now her energy supplier cannot find any outstanding bill.
- Miraculously healed from leg pain! – When she attended the miracle service she was experiencing severe pain in her knees. I was prophesying and I went and laid hands on her and she was instantly HEALED!

Some other headlines are "Delivered from drugs and alcohol", "Man uses miracle pack to prosper in business", "Status granted", "Money cometh", "Instant healing". In this edition of 'The Miracle Times' there are around thirty-five miraculous interventions of which ten involve healing. The question often asked is how does healing occur? There is general agreement that it requires faith (and desire) but whose faith? There is the divine will, the person needing a cure or healing and the person being used as a catalyst for that healing: sometimes a physician, sometimes a clinician, sometimes the clergy and sometimes the member of the church. Does healing depend on the faith of all three, two out of three or just one?

Recently my brother was diagnosed with life-limiting lung cancer, and we were told to prepare for his premature death. A number of us prayed for complete healing, including our nephew who is a member of another faith tradition. On his next hospital visit, my brother was told that his condition had been downgraded and that the lump was a carcinoid that would respond to surgery and should not cause him long term problems. Was he cured? After surgery and convalescence he is well on the road to full health although missing the upper lobe of one lung, but with sensible lifestyle choices and medication, his illness should not now limit his life expectation. Could we claim a miracle has occurred? I doubt that we could ever truly know the divine will, but our prayers urge in us the compassion that God has for His creation. Mediated by the Holy Spirit and calling on the name of Jesus, we plead for the healing of those who seek recovery. Did those of us who prayed for my brother believe that he would be fully healed? Did my brother think our prayers would have any effect? These are very difficult answers to give. In hindsight, of course, I knew that God would act, and I can point toward the living proof and the medical records that evidence my brother's healing, but he still had a disease and required surgery and there were some complications before we could be sure of his restoration. He will live with less lung capacity for the rest of his life so can we really claim full healing? What would be truly miraculous is if the lung grew back to its original size and the scar under his right armpit disappeared.

What is more concerning is when there is no apparent answer to prayer. A man that I regularly met in a residential care home would tell me that he could not become a Christian or believe in a God that allows children to suffer all around the world; a God that allows natural disasters like tsunamis, earthquakes, hurricanes, floods and droughts to take pure and innocent life; a God that fails to stop murder, rape and mob violence; a God that allows evil to prosper unchecked. I would counter his list of depravity pointing toward the love shared in family, neighbourhood and community; the good works of faith-based aid agencies and organizations; the common humanity that respects, encourages and enables people to flourish and grow; and the moral standards that the greater majority live by. I never convinced him and he died. At his funeral I delivered a message of Christian hope that he gained the wisdom he needed to understand the workings of God's mind – for His ways are not ours. Was he healed? No hindsight will allow me to see into the Kingdom of God to glimpse whether the man embraced that final prayer, so my own faith in the eternal life is the only thing on which I can rely.

In this book we are concentrating on miraculous healings performed by Jesus and how those who witnessed and observed the event were healed as a result. Rarely, I suspect, were those people healed of a physical disease, and we have already established that there is no way of knowing what resulted from Jesus' actions. We are using imagination and a reader-response technique in an attempt to get to the hidden voice within the text. The contemporary example above of my brother's healing might not be considered a miracle on the biblical scale, but there was much rejoicing in our household and a weight of concern did lift from my shoulders when we learnt that he would remain with us for a while longer. In that sense it was a *healing beyond the miracle*, and it has further encouraged me to approach the subject matter of this book with greater intensity.

In our next study we look at the healing of the demon-possessed (possibly epileptic) boy recorded by all three of the synoptic (definition: taking a common view) Gospel writers. (Mark 9:1-4, Matthew 17:14-21, Luke 9:37-43) It is the most specific miracle that speaks of faith. In all three accounts the healing is preceded by 'The Transfiguration', when Jesus and three disciples ascend the mountain and encounter God in the cloud and the figures of Elijah and Moses are seen in consort with Jesus. Matthew's account of the healing story shortens Mark's version in order to focus attention on the unbelief of the disciples. He is getting the reader to view Jesus' descent in the same manner of Moses' before him (Exodus 32).

As Moses came down from the mountain with two tablets of stone on which the Ten Commandments were written, the people had turned away from their trust and beliefs. Jesus was confronted by a crowd who watched as the remaining nine disciples were unable to help the man who brought his demon-possessed child for a cure. We know that they had had experience and success in the past (Matthew 10:1ff) so why did the disciples struggle on this occasion? Matthew's account concludes that the disciples had little faith; in fact they are accused of 'no faith', for even if they had had faith the size of a mustard seed it would have enabled them to move mountains.

The father of the boy pleaded to Jesus for mercy, linking his request not only to the cure of his son's condition but to the stronger request for his son to be saved. The elements of fire and water were likely to be shorthand references used by Matthew to alert the reader to a wider context that is largely lost to us today. Mark's version of the miracle adds that this was the man's only son. His central point is that the generation is faithless and perverse, referring not only to the disciples but those who had come to see what the disciples *could not* do rather than the things that Jesus *could*. There is allusion back to the people of Moses' time (Deuteronomy 32:5) who were a warped and crooked generation. Only in this version do the people respond with astonishment at Jesus' actions.

Mark gives his reader the fullest account of this story and highlights the lack of faith from different characters. There is a great crowd around the nine disciples who did not join Jesus, Peter, James and John up the mountain. As Jesus arrives the crowd turns to him and are "immediately overcome with awe". Perhaps he radiated the glory of God after his mountaintop experience, or maybe there was such exasperation among the people that they were excited to see him. This is almost the last occasion that Mark records Jesus performing a healing; only Bartimaeus receives this ministry before Jesus is arrested in the garden of Gethsemane, when the slave's ear is severed.

Jesus defuses the situation by asking them about the argument. The father explains that he had brought his son for healing but the disciples were unable to help him. The Apostle Peter's firsthand account recorded by Mark puts the same words on the lips of Jesus that are repeated with minor variations by Matthew and Luke: "You faithless generation, how much longer must I be among you? How much longer must I put up with you? Bring him to me." Jesus is referring to the faithlessness of the age, the people and his own followers. As the boy is brought the symptoms described by the father earlier are now evident, and in response to Jesus' supplementary question to the father we learn that it has afflicted him since childhood. We also learnt more about its devastating effects. A clue to finding the *healing beyond the miracle* appears when the father asks Jesus to, "have pity on us and help us." It is the boy that is the primary sufferer, but such is the disease that others are caused to suffer non-physical effects as a result.

Jesus then challenges the faith of the father: "If you are able! – All things can be done for the one who believes."

The father cries out in reply, "I believe; help my unbelief!"

The child is cured but not before what seems to be a near death experience, according to Mark. The father is further tested in his belief as the boy cries out and convulses violently before collapsing into a copse-like position, such that most thought him dead. We are not told whether there is a dramatic pause, but the narrative says that Jesus takes hold of his hand and lifts him up to a standing position. Only after the event and in private do the disciples ask why they were unable to heal the boy.

"This kind can come out only through prayer [and fasting according to some manuscripts of Matthew's gospel]"

According to Edwards this is the first injunction to prayer in Mark's Gospel. He rightly identifies prayer as the focus and direction of faith in specific requests to God. He writes, "Both faith and prayer testify that spiritual power is not in oneself but in God alone and both wait in trust upon his promise to save." Quoting Grundmann he notes that, "prayer is faith turned to God" [42]

Earlier in the commentary – and referring specifically to the faith of the father – he says:

> *True faith is always aware how small and inadequate it is. The father becomes a believer not when he amasses a sufficient quantum of faith but when he risks everything on what little faith he has, when he yields his insufficiency to the sufficiency of Jesus, 'I do believe; help me overcome my unbelief'. The risk of faith is more costly to the father than bringing his son to Jesus, for he can talk about his son but he must 'cry out' for faith. True faith takes no confidence in itself, nor does it judge Jesus by the weakness of his followers. It looks to the One More Powerful (Mark 1:7) who stands in the place of God, whose authoritative word restores life from chaos. True faith is unconditional openness to God, a decision in the face of all to the contrary that Jesus is able.* [43]

"The sole bridge between frail humanity and the all sufficiency of God is faith," [44] and the transport for that faith is prayer (and fasting). The Gospel writers all go in different directions following their accounts of this miracle. Mark describes Jesus' teaching on servant leadership, Matthew tells of the miracle of the fish that swallows the four drachma temple tax and Luke concentrates on Jesus' passion prediction. The writers give us scant detail about the effect of these episodes on the lives of others. The disciples of 'little faith' (Matthew 6:30, 8:26, 14:31, 16:8) show even less on the occasion on Jesus' arrest and at the time of his resurrection. Despite the clear teaching given here and on other occasions about the power available to those who have faith, the disciples remained diffident. What of the other characters in this story: the boy, his father (and mother), the crowd, the scribes, Jesus the Son, and the Father? Moving from disappointment at the inaction of the disciples to universal astonishment at the greatness of God is quite a leap and

---

[42] James R Edwards. *The Pillar New Testament Commentary on Mark*. Apollos 2002, p281
[43] Ibid., p280
[44] Ibid., p280

must surely have had an effect on someone other than the son and his father.

Let me conclude this chapter with an article from 'The Miracle Times' – it highlights the efficacy of witnessing miracles in a modern setting communicated by testimony – although I believe that our faith is not intended as a means to personal gain and benefit. Personally I would argue that the person of faith is the carrier of other's care and concerns, hopes and dreams, rather than a depository for God's treasures. By now I hope the reader is able to imagine a story from the scripture that might gain insight into the biblical story we have studied.

A friend brought me to church and straight away I knew it was different because it was equipped with the word of God and I could see it in practice. My coming to the ministry was not a direct cause of problem I was facing although I had situations in my life that did not seem to and I felt this overwhelming hunger to know more about God. I had been to a lot of other churches but upon coming to this ministry I felt welcome. I felt at ease and for the first time in my life I experienced this astounding peace as I learnt more about His Word. I also learnt how to apply it to my own life and actively use the word of God like a day-to-day manual. The word of God says that He is the same yesterday, today and forever more and this really is true.

I could finally see that the miracles he performed centuries ago he could still do the same for me. However what is lacking is our disbelief and refusal to acknowledge His power. But God is omniscient and omnipotent and there is nothing that is impossible through Him. I could really see through all the testimonies here at church and it is so wonderful how everyone loves God and acknowledges him through the sharing of their testimonies. When I became a member of the church, everything in my life changed and so did my outlook on the situations and circumstances I faced in my everyday life. It came to a point where I reacted positively to the storms that came because now I knew I could make it, because I was able to identify that this happens not just to me but to others as well and that often it's normal.

What keeps me going on and strengthens you is the spiritual guidance that you receive from the ministry because it equips you to face the challenges that come your way. God has also shown me his grace and mercy in my life, I went to court and the situation was so hopeless because I was guilty and deserved the harshest punishment possible. Surprisingly though the judge kept asking me is there anything that I can do to help you and turn this around for your sake. I really thank God for his ministry because if it was not for the prayers only God knows where I would be now but his favour pulled me through.

God then showed me another great miracle, I was driving in the snow and I stopped the car but for some reason it kept on going. I tried to come out of the car but I had my children with me as well. The car kept going, it hit a curb, started skidding and rolling backwards and forwards and then it just landed on its side. Miraculously my children and I walked out the car with no bruises; not even a single scratch on us. This is just another of the many miracles God does for me every day, every second, but its only when we learn to tap into that anointing that it all becomes possible. I do not know what could have happened to me and my children if I was not praying. But in the midst of the accident I wasn't scared or thinking I'm going to die. I just thought to myself, "oh the car is rolling," and I kept on praying for I knew 'Greater is He that is in me than he that is in the world'.

Listening to the church's teachers I am able to understand the word of God with depth and wisdom and now I know I am blessed and highly favoured. And I keep receiving favour all the time... Testimonies are so important as there is nothing too small or too little in God's eyes and I love how the ministry emphasizes this. The word of God in Revelation 12:11 says that, "we overcome the devil by the blood of the lamb and the words of our testimonies."

I have always been prayerful but I could never settle in a church and moved from one church to the other. My prayer to God always used to be to have a church where I could call home and I found my place here... It's so important to find a place where the leaders will be able to help you develop spiritually, guide you, uplift you and encourage you to persevere. I have found a home here, the place where the Captives are set free and souls refreshed. [45]

Well that church may not be everyone's idea of the ideal home but the author of that article has found her faith strengthened. If faith is the bridge between humanity and God and prayer is the transport, who are we to say that her action and this church are not a glimpse and foretaste of the Kingdom of God?

---

[45] 'The Miracle Times' is edited by Kyla Cadorin on behalf of The Kingdom Church. Their website is www.bishopclimate.org

CHAPTER TEN

Come Out and Sit Up

During ordination training I needed to earn money to support our young family through college. Following a placement with a funeral company, I was retained on a casual temporary contract of employment. Most of the time I drove the funeral transport and carried the deceased into church for the funeral service, but after-hours I was on call to collect the deceased and transport them to the mortuary. I recall one night having to assist a funeral director in an operation on a dead person to remove a pacemaker. As the person was to be cremated this was necessary to avoid an explosion within the cremator from the batteries overheating in the chamber.

The procedure should have been carried out earlier but had been forgotten so we were operating on this person around midnight. I remember the night very well as a storm was raging and the wind was whistling through the mortuary and thunder and lightning were exploding and flashing all around the building. By this stage in my undertaking career I had seen many things and was reasonably comfortable around death, but this night remains etched into my memory as one of the most frightening events in my life. I suspect the reader is already picturing the scene of two suited men with scalpel in hand and kidney dish posed ready to perform the procedure. Dead bodies can twitch as muscles spasm and relax, they can make sounds as trapped air releases over vocal cords and out of other orifices, though generally they do not do either of these unless the body is being moved about. Before the reader makes up their own horror story of fantasy let me say now that none of this, and nothing else, happened; the pacemaker removal was effected without fuss and with respect for the cadaver that had the implant. It did not, however, feel that easy, and I was petrified that the person would sit up and tell us off for violating his body at any moment.

Zombies, werewolves and vampires are the stuff of horror movies, making us hide behind the settee. The public has a fascination for the possibility that there is life after death, but it is rarely portrayed as a welcomed reality and in faith terms it is often spiritualized and theologized. How different is the present day from the first century view of such things? The Bible contains seven stories of people being resurrected, of which four involve children being restored to their parent(s). Elijah raises the Zarephath widow's son (1Kings 17:17-24); Elisha raises the Shunammite's son (2 Kings 4:18-37); and Jesus raises Jairus' daughter and the Nain widow's son. After Jesus' own resurrection, his follower Peter raises Tabitha (translated as Dorcas in Acts 9:36-43), leaving one other: the raising of Lazarus. In this chapter we will concentrate on the raising of the Nain widow's son, only record by Luke (7:11-17), and the raising of Lazarus, only recorded by John (11:1-44). These two differ from the third resurrection miracle performed by Jesus in that Jairus' daughter lay on her bed and was only recently deceased when raised, whereas the Nain widow's son was being carried out of the town for burial and Lazarus had been in the funeral tomb for four days. Any attempt to suggest the last two only appeared dead and that these were resuscitations can be ruled out, in my view. However, we believe that death is irreversible so it is not surprising that we attempt to rationalise these stories in order to understand them.

The reader decides what is possible and what is impossible and then approaches the text in a manner that reflects their personal beliefs and opinions. If disbelief is suspended the story will yield one set of possibilities that failure to do will not. This is the essence of reader-response criticism and puts the reader in control of interpretation. However, the writer will present the material in such a way as to encourage or discourage literal acceptance of the text as and when required. The fusion of these two intentions will result in the understanding of the story being formulated. From this perspective different and sometimes opposing interpretations may result, but I argue that these cannot be reconciled by the biblical criticism previously employed, which means we are left with contradictions.

The prior question relating specifically to the two miracles considered here is whether it is possible to be healed from death. Should they even be considered healing miracles? A recent popular science fiction series ('Torchwood: Miracle Day') depicts a time when no human alive on the planet is able to die. People are shot, strangled, blown up, have heart attacks and fatal road traffic accidents... but they cannot die. The people feel the pain and suffer... but they cannot die. It is soon calculated that within four months the resulting growth in the world's population will cause catastrophic shortages in the food supply, and energy supplies and amenities will cease... but still the people will not die. The rest of the series and therefore the answer to this global problem were still to be aired at the time of writing.

Again, the question is whether sustained life when death is 'cheated' can be considered a healing. I prefer to view Jesus' resurrection miracles as rebirths rather than healings and consider that the person whom Jesus brings back to life would never be able to live as they did before they died and, of course, one day the person reborn has to die. I admit that the story of Jairus' daughter does not give me such major concerns. However we describe the miracles involving the widow's son and Lazarus they are powerful and had great impact.

Let us consider Luke's story first. It has parallels with the story of Elijah in Zarephath in that both he and Jesus come to a town, meet a widow, heal her son and are acclaimed for their work. Elijah is called a man of God and Jesus heralded as a great prophet. Both are seen as glorifying God. The accounts differ more than they compare though. Jesus does not have prior knowledge of the widow and has not lived with her or relied on her hospitality. The Nainian widow does not plead for restoration of her son, and Jesus performs the miracle out of compassion, not in response to petition. The manner of the healing is different as well. Elijah's miracle takes place in private, and he prays three times and lies over the body, whereas Jesus speaks a word and the young man sits up. In both accounts the subject of the miracle is "given to his mother" (Luke 7:15 cf. 1 Kings 17:23). Luke is keen to emphasise that this is the widow's only child, something he does again in the Jairus story (8:42) and in that of the (possibly) epileptic boy (9:38). The context of Luke's account places it in the heart of Jesus' Galilean ministry. It follows the healing of the centurion's servant and precedes Jesus' conversation with the disciples of John the Baptist who are sent to ask whether he is 'the one'. Jesus sends them back to John with a message:

Luke 7:22-23
The blind receive sight, the lame walk, those with leprosy are cured, the deaf hear, the dead are raised and the good news is preached to the poor. Blessed is the man who does not fall away on account of me.

We can only speculate why Luke has ordered his writings as they are, but this story is exclusive to the writer alone. Perhaps he is trying to validate his messages to the existing followers of John the Baptist.

It will be difficult to suggest who receives *healing beyond the miracle* because there is likely to be a level of trauma to deal with first when the young man sits up from his funeral bier or Lazarus appears at the entrance to the cave. As a former pallbearer, I can imagine my reaction to a copse coming to life, and I struggle to comprehend the healing it would bring. Perhaps after further reflection I might consider the second chance resurrection offers. I would certainly be seized with fear, but whether I would then glorify God is extremely speculative. The healing that the mother enjoys, after burying her husband and seeing her son die and come back to life, is interesting. What would that look like? Nain is a small village on the slopes of Mount Tabor in Galilee, about five miles southeast of Nazareth. This would explain why the people conclude that Jesus serves his own but does not adequately support the word about him spreading throughout Judea as this little village is over the northern borders of that region. Perhaps the wider healing was the spread of Jesus' fame and associated ministry to the marginalised in society.

The second miracle has a greater sense of intimacy as it is a story about friends and intense emotional relationships. In the widow's story Jesus was moved by what he saw, whereas with Lazarus he is challenged by Martha and Mary because of his absence. Luke introduces us to the family (10:38-42) and the different personalities of the two women. John tells us that Mary is the woman who anointed Jesus with a pint of pure nard in an incident recorded after the raising of her brother (12:3). Whether Jesus had their brother in mind when telling the parable of the rich man and Lazarus (Luke 16:19-31) is debated because the name was common in Hebrew circles. It is possible that John knew of the parable when writing his Gospel and this story of Lazarus' resurrection. John tells us that Jesus is going to use Lazarus' illness to glorify God and bring glory to himself (11:4).

By staying another two days where he was rather than travelling to Bethany, the home of his friends, was Jesus making sure that the impact of this miracle would be sensational? This was the last miracle recorded by John before Jesus rose from his own death. In context, it precedes (and is given as the reason for) the Sanhedrin's meeting and plot to kill Jesus, forcing him to retreat from Jerusalem and stay in a village called Ephraim.

Even before the disciples set out to go to Bethany, Jesus makes it clear that Lazarus is dead. His purpose is to make them believe. Thomas' morbid response is that going to Judea, where the people have already tried to stone Jesus (10:31) and in particular going to the home of Lazarus, is likely to lead to their own death. His ironic aside (11:16) will later become a fulfilled prophesy for Jesus. The news of Lazarus' death is no surprise to Jesus, and when Martha meets him she proclaims her faith in his abilities but reflects that he has arrived too late. He adjures her to believe and delivers the now iconic line, "I am the resurrection and the life..." and asks, "Do you believe?"

Martha declares her faith and returns home to fetch Mary. Jesus gets angry when she admonishes his tardiness and requests to be taken to where the tomb is situated. Fighting back the tears he asks for the stone to be rolled away, against Martha protestations and questioning her belief once again. For the sake of the crowd so that they might believe, Jesus shouts into the cave, "Lazarus, come out!" and he appears bound in cloth which Jesus instructs should be removed. As a result, many of the Jews put their faith in him.

The healing that many experienced that day was a cure of their unbelief. In the previous chapter, we suggested that faith was a bridge between humanity and God with prayer as the transportation. Belief is perhaps the intention to make the journey in the first place. The Nicene Creed enables worshippers collectively to affirm what we, the Christian Church, believe. The Apostles' Creed encourages the individual to assert what "I believe..." Jesus begins this miracle from a distance knowing that he wants to teach and illustrate the importance of a person's belief for miraculous events to take place. If we want extraordinary things to happen we have to have extraordinary belief that they will. Tepid faith and timid belief might cost us our eternal life. As Jesus said, "...everyone who believes in me will never die."

In a shameless recasting of the Wizard of Oz let us attempt to illustrate what happens when a person gains the belief of a characteristic that everyone else sees but a lack of belief prevents the person accepting it is within them.

Peter was tending his nets and mumbling to himself about his lack of skill in communicating to people, "Why can't I work out what to say and recognise the good in other people?"

He was just about to get up a good head of self deprecating steam when a man called Jesus said, "Why don't you come with me? I'm going to see God, he will help you!"

The two of them went on their way until they came across two more fishermen called James and John who were arguing about which one of them was the best. "Stop your arguing," Jesus said. "Do you want to follow me? God will be able to sort out your squabbling."

I could see that Mr. Zebedee appreciated this intervention, and the four of them travelled a little further until they saw a man on the roadside with his head in his hands rocking backwards and forwards.

"What's the matter?" Peter asked.

"I'm so confused and don't know who or what to believe; can you help?

"No", I said, "but we are on our way to see God with Jesus here. I am sure he can help; do you want to come?"

"Yes please."

"What is your name, by the way?"

"My name is Thomas and I am a twin, I think."

The five of them travelled together, but Thomas would always lag behind the rest, forever questioning whether he was doing the right thing. It was probably because he hung back that he wasn't with the others when Jesus asked who people said he was. (Peter was brilliant on this day but still didn't realise he had a great way of talking to people and getting the best out of them. He said that Jesus was the Christ. Jesus told him not to tell anyone about him because he wanted them to come to that belief themselves. Even then Peter thought he needed to see God so that he could get the gift he needed personally.) Thomas also missed the time that the other ascended a mountain and Jesus' clothes went dazzling white. Peter was so enthusiastic again and Jesus hoped he was beginning to believe in himself.

They all went to stay at Peter's house in Capernaum, and as usual James and John were arguing about who was the greatest. In the end Jesus called everyone together and said, "If anyone wants to be first, he must be the last and the servant of all." Then he took a little child and had him stand among them. Taking him in his arms, he said to them, "Whoever welcomes one of these little children in my name welcomes me; and whoever welcomes me does not welcome me but the one who sent me."

The "brothers of thunder", as they got nicknamed because of their arguing, still didn't understand or believe what Jesus was telling them. A little later, their mother got in on the act. Just before the followers went into Jerusalem she sidled up to Jesus and asked if her boys could be on the right and left of him in the kingdom. Jesus explained politely that she didn't know what she was asking, but then the boys arrived and boasted that they could drink from the same cup as Jesus. The rest of the disciples were annoyed about this so Jesus gathered them all together and said again, "Whoever wants to become great among you must be your servant and whoever wants to be first must be your slave – just as the Son of Man did not come to be served but to serve and to give his life as a ransom for many."

That got the message home; the brothers acted as one and went on to become great leaders, but first they wanted to hear what God had to say. Thomas continued to ask questions all the time and was growing in belief but would never let on.

The group was asked to go to Bethany to visit Lazarus who was ill. Although Jesus said he would, they waited for two days before setting off.

"Why are we going there?" Thomas asked Jesus.

"Our friend has fallen asleep; but I am going to wake him up." Jesus replied.

"Why are we going all that way just to wake him up? You know they try to stone you there. Besides it will be dark soon and it is a long way." Thomas moaned and groaned.

Jesus then dropped a bombshell. "Lazarus is dead, and for your sake I am glad I was not there, so that you may believe. But let us go to him."

In a fit of petulant reproach Thomas called out to the others, "Let us also go, that we may die with him." Nevertheless as they walked along he thought on what Jesus has said, and one day his own belief would be sorely tested.

In less than two weeks, their leader had been arrested, tried, convicted and crucified, and the disciples took refuge in a locked room. Thomas missed the first time Jesus appeared to the followers and as usual questioned their account. He didn't question the next appearance when Jesus invited him to put his fingers into the palms of his hands or put his hand into his side. As Thomas said himself, "My Lord and my God." From that point no one heard Thomas voice any doubts. All his questions were answered.

A little while after, seven of the disciples (including the four I have mentioned) were fishing in Tiberias and Jesus arrived to make breakfast and share it with them. After they had eaten Jesus took Peter aside and asked him three times whether he loved him. Each time he said, "Yes," and because he spoke so well and understood so many things Jesus asked him one more thing: "Follow me?"

All four of the disciples – Peter, James, John and Thomas – believed and found the God-given gifts that they had always possessed. They just needed Jesus to help them find them. And as for Jesus?

He took them back to Bethany and lifted his hands to bless them. While he was blessing them, he left them and was taken up into heaven.

No Toto I am afraid, but a deliberate play on the familiar classic to illustrate that the miracles we considered in this chapter are difficult to read for a *healing beyond the miracle* unless we attest to the possibility of them having greatest effect on the disciples themselves. I accept that most of the healing miracles will have had an impact on the disciples, but I have chosen the two resurrection stories and added Jesus' appearances in the creative writing to seek out the possible greater effect these miracles had on them. The reader is free to respond according to their approach.

CHAPTER ELEVEN

The Remainder

In this final chapter we shall investigate the remaining healing miracles not considered elsewhere. Mark (14:47-48) and Matthew (26:51-52) describe the aggression that results in the slave's ear being cut off by someone who drew a sword. John (18:10-11) tells us that the 'someone' is Peter and names the slave as Malchus. It is only Luke (22:49-51) that attests a healing when Jesus touches his ear. It is one of the few occasions when all four Gospel writers record an event. This contrast reminds us that the writers had different purposes and intended different readerships. Twelftree concludes:

> *At the risk of seeming simplistic, in Mark, the earliest Gospel, Jesus is the miracle worker who teaches and must suffer. In Matthew, Jesus is the teacher who also performs miracles. Luke carefully balances Jesus' ministry of word and deed. Not so John (and the Fourth Gospel). Here Jesus is in such communion with and is to be so identified with, God that he is first and foremost the author of the most stupendous wonders which are signs of his unmistakable identity, origin and destiny seen pre-eminently in the sign of his death and resurrection.* [46]

It will benefit those who wish to take a reader-response view on biblical text further to learn from the other criticisms who the intended reader might have been for the Gospel writers. It is too general to say that Mark wrote to Gentiles and Matthew wrote to Jews, with John writing in defence of the Christian faith against

---

[46] Graham H. Twelftree. *Jesus: The Miracle Worker.* Illinois, InterVarsity Press 1999 p 343

Gnostics, but it is a starting place. However, knowing the intended reader will not necessarily make you the ideal reader or the preferred reader. It will make you an informed reader, and I hope that by now this book is encouraging and inspiring you to read the Bible with a different perspective – eager to investigate the hidden aspects of the writer's intention.

The four remaining miracles not previously considered are:

- The healing of the deaf mute
  Mark 7:31-37   No parallels

- The healing of the bent woman
  Luke 13:10-17   No parallels

- The healing of the man with dropsy
  Luke 14:1-6   No parallels

- The healing by the Sheep Gate
  John 5:2-18   No parallels

We might have included Mark's recorded miracle with his story of the healing of the blind man which we considered in Chapter Four, as there is a message that Jesus makes by bringing the two together. In response to the disciples' continued lack of faith and understanding, he admonishes them by saying, "Do you have eyes and fail to see and ears and fail to hear?" The context of the reading is placed in Jesus' Gentile ministry following his encounter with the Syrophoenician woman in Tyre, in the region of the Decapolis (Ten Cities), north of Galilee and Capernaum. It is the same area where Jesus cured the demoniac (Chapter Seven) and precedes a feeding miracle and the healing of the blind man at Bethsaida. Mark may have had Isaiah's oracle of judgement against Jerusalem in mind in recording this healing of a death mute, which is unique to his Gospel. The prophet concludes his warning with a note of optimism:

> Isaiah 35:5-6
> *[The] eyes of the blind will be opened and the ears of the deaf unstopped. Then will the lame leap like a deer and the mute tongue shout for joy...*

This is clearly not a life-threatening or limiting disease, and the man is brought to Jesus by the crowd who beg him to lay hands on him. This short foray into Gentile territory must have been successful and highly effective given the crowd's expectations of a cure. In private, Jesus treats the man with touch, saliva, prayer and command, and the man is immediately able to hear and speak. Jesus' order given to the crowd to keep silent about the healing falls on death ears, and they proclaim the miracle with zeal. Such was the impact on the crowd that they were astounded. The dictionary definition of 'astound' [47] suggests this is an intensification of 'astonish', a word more often used to describe the crowd's reaction to Jesus' healing miracles. Mark intensifies the reaction still further saying that they were "astounded beyond measure". The only other occasion in the New Testament where we are told of a similar reaction in the crowd is when Peter heals a crippled beggar (Acts 3:11). For our purposes, we might reasonably expect that the miracle created healings beyond Jesus' actions, given the response of the crowd to the miracle. The only glimpse we can get of these possible reactions is by the use of creative imagination.

We now move to the remaining two healing miracles in Luke, one involving a crippled woman and the other a man with dropsy. Both stories are located on Jesus' journey from Galilee to Jerusalem, the first during his teaching in Judea and the second as he begins a meal at a Pharisee's house. Of the eighteen recorded healing miracles in Luke's Gospel there are only three that appear after these two, which in turn make up half of the four miracles unique to the writer. Between the two miracles are Jesus' warnings about non-acceptance of his message and his lament over Jerusalem. The parable of the great banquet, the cost of discipleship and the three 'lost' parables follow the second miracle we are considering. Taken as a whole section, the purpose of the narrative is to persuade the people by word and deed the need to accept his message and acclaim that, "Blessed is he who comes in the name of the Lord." (Luke 13:35b)

The first miracle takes place in a synagogue on the Sabbath, a scene that we have considered in Chapter Six and, like the man with a withered hand we considered there, the woman in this story does not appear to have come to the synagogue seeking a cure but is used by Jesus to challenge the authorities. It is the last occasion that Jesus preaches in a synagogue accordingly to Luke's writings. The point

---

[47] Oxford Dictionary of English on Apple v2.2.1

that Jesus makes to the leaders of the synagogue is that a daughter of Abraham, bound for eighteen years, is untied and given water. The number used is rare, and I can only suggest one possible parallel found in the book of Judges (10:8) being the length of time under Philistine oppression following the Israelites 'evil in the eyes of the Lord.' Whether this oracle that records God's punishment on the people for worshipping other gods is connected with the woman bent over for a similar period is speculative. It can be supported by the author's use of the term "put to shame" which echoes the same expression used by Isaiah (45:6) admonishing the people for their "making of idols." It may however be too much to suggest that the phrase "the entire crowd was rejoicing at all the wonderful things that he was doing" is a deliberate parallel to the reaction of the people to Moses bringing them the second set of commandments – although it is there! (Exodus 34:10)

Biblical exploration can, and has, lead to some highly questionable interpretations of scripture however plausible. My hope is that using a reader-response approach will liberate the reader from other criticisms that require textual, literary and historical reference points. It is right to locate interpretation of Jesus' healing miracles within a broadly acceptable tradition of understanding, but I believe we can also allow imagination to enable the reader to gain experiential insights as well. This work deliberately tries to find the *healing beyond the miracle* and concentrates on finding the hidden characters of the stories. For example, we might find the sinister and secretive opponent to Jesus beyond the Temple authorities that are traditionally held in contempt. Reader-response may also allow us to imagine setting and context, enabling the interpreter to add colour and texture to the story.

The meal and sharing food in hospitality is an important setting for Luke (5:29, 33, 7:34, 36, 9:10, 10:8, 38, 11:2, 12:37, 14:1, 15, 15:23, 19:6, 22:14, 24:30) [48] so it is not surprising that the next healing miracle appears in that context (Luke 14:1-6). It is an invitation from a Pharisee to eat a meal on the Sabbath, but there is another agenda as Jesus is being closely watched.

---

[48] For further reading. Tim Chester, *A Meal with Jesus: Discover Grace*, Community and Mission around the Table. Crossway 2011

A man with 'dropsy' appeared in front of Jesus, and the way Luke introduces this character suggests he was a deliberate 'plant' put there to test Jesus' reactions. The best description I found was that 'dropsy' referred to the symptom of body swelling caused by an accumulation of fluid in the body cavities and tissue space as a result of a disease of the heart, liver or kidney, for example. I suspect that we would all be put off our meal if a large fluid-retained man stood in front of us as we were going in for dinner. Bearing that picture in mind, how would you now deliver the line, "Is it lawful to cure people on the Sabbath, or not?" The way the reader expresses that question will have an impact on the silent response of the hosts.

No wonder Jesus sent him away after healing the man of blob! The defence of retrieving a child or an ox from a well had a hint of subtle humour in my reading of the story, and I was not surprised that the hosts could not reply – they did not know what to say. My Jesus was smiling at this point, and many around the edge of the scene were chuckling at what had just happened. I tried to find some images that depict the scene, but the great artists do not appear to have made this healing a subject of their work. Perhaps a form of reader-response criticism might be used to draw or paint the scene that the reader imagines.

Our last healing miracle is from John's Gospel (5:2-18 with explanation in 5:19-47) involving a paralytic waiting for thirty eight years to get into the angel whirlpool at Bethzatha (Hebrew), Bethesda (Aramaic) or yet another variation Bethsaida. The reference to angelic influence and different place names introduces the reader to another challenge in reading scripture. Not all the manuscripts from which our Bibles are translated are the same. Before printing presses and mass reproduction was possible, handwritten scrolls were produced by people copying text from existing documents. Errors were made, which is why in the margin of many Bibles there are references like, "Some manuscripts Bethzatha; other manuscripts Bethsaida." [49] In the version used for this miracle, verse 4 is omitted, but a footnote says, "From time to time an angel of the Lord would come down and stir up the waters. The first one into the pool after each such disturbance would be cured of whatever disease he had." Was the

---

[49] New Internation Version, Hodder and Stoughton 1996

copyist dissatisfied with the original text and wanted to add clarity and justification to the story? The additional verse that is generally unaccepted by translators does add movement and drama to the miracle.

The description of the five porticoes and naming the entrance to the pool adds additional depth to the imaginary picture. Nehemiah was responsible for the rebuilding of Jerusalem and the Temple along with Ezra before him. The Sheep Gate in mentioned in his account. (3:1, 32, 12:39) I suspect that "thirty eight years" means 'a long time', but it might refer to the number of years of wilderness exodus between Kadesh Barnea and the Zered Valley (Deuteronomy 2:14) as these are the only two verses where that number is used. The contrast between this paralytic and the man found in the other Gospels (see Chapter Three) is stark. This man had no friends to help, but his faith made him believe that if he could just get into that pool (before anyone else) he could be made well. Similar to the other healing, Jesus simply told him to get up, take his mat and walk. Thirty eight years of waiting were over in an instant, and he did as he was told. The healing appears to have taken place without many witnesses, if any, because it is only when he was caught carrying his mat that he was challenged by the Jews, and Jesus had managed to disappear into the crowd. It is only later that the man convicted Jesus following a subsequent encounter that Jesus engineered. Only then did Jesus get the chance, in John's telling of the story, to theologise and sermonize to the authorities. The effect of the healing was in the opportunity it offered Jesus to preach to the religious officials. Whether any were challenged and moved by his teaching we are not told.

It might be possible to imagine a story that brings these four (or five) final healing miracles together, but it is probably not advisable. Instead I want to give a brief review of Richard Bauckham's book, 'Jesus and the Eyewitnesses'. [50] The Bishop of Durham, N. T. Wright commends the book on the flysheet saying,

> *The question of whether the Gospels are based on eyewitness accounts has long been controversial. Now Richard Bauckham, in a characteristic tour de force, draws in his unparalleled*

---

[50] Richard Bauckham. *Jesus and the Eyewitnesses: The Gospels as Eyewitness Testimony*. Grand Rapids, Michigan: William B. Eerdmans Publishing Company 2006

knowledge of the world of the First Christian to argue not only that the Gospels do indeed contain eyewitness testimony but that their first readers would certainly have recognized them as such...

Bauckham is dissatisfied with the direction of scholarship in its quest to uncover the historical Jesus, suggesting that...

...the enterprise of attempting to reconstruct the historical figure of Jesus in a way that is ... free of the concerns of faith and dogma, has been highly problematic for Christian faith and theology. [51]

He suggests we need to recover the sense in which the Gospels are testimony and defends the approach:

Trusting testimony is not an irrational act of faith that leaves critical rationality aside; it is, on the contrary, the rationally appropriate way of responding to authentic testimony. [52]

His approach is a little different to reader-response criticism as it concentrates on the writer, or recorder, of the eyewitness accounts. It does not include the approach that a reader might have. Bauckham speaks of the anonymous community that, through oral tradition, transmitted the eyewitness accounts during the lifetime of the eyewitnesses and how their testimony became written accounts within a short time. In a chapter on names in the Gospel tradition, he considers why some characters are named while others remain anonymous. He concludes that those named are the people who become the eyewitnesses. Bauckham contends that...

...the role of named individuals in the formulation and transmission of traditions of Jesus' words and deeds largely disappeared ... as a result of the form-critical movement in Gospel scholarship in the early twentieth century. [53]

In summary, Bauckham argues:

The Gospels put us in close touch with the eyewitnesses of the historical Jesus.

---

[51] Ibid., p2
[52] Ibid., p5
[53] Ibid., p93

The book is a slight diversion for us as it deals with the text without the reader, as I say above. However it is a useful excursion as it helps us to think about the validity of the original text, the healing miracle stories, from which we attempt to imagine our way beyond, in order to uncover other resulting healings.

The prior question that I attempt to answer at this late stage in this book is: why did Jesus perform healing miracles? The response is significant as it influences our view on whom they were intended for and for what purpose.

- To excite wonder in the observers
- To reflect the glory of God
- To reflect the compassionate nature of Jesus
- To carry a message
- To be a sign to Israel
- To build up faith and belief

Or as Paul claims:

1 Corinthians 1:22
The Jews demand miraculous signs and the Greek look for wisdom.

I suggest that none of the miracles were performed solely to heal the person and that all the miracles had effect beyond the sufferer. There are obvious examples like Peter and company following his mother-in-law's recovery, Jairus, the nobleman, the centurion, the widow at Nain, the father of the (possibly) epileptic son, the friends of the paralytic, the Syrophoenician's mother, Mary and Martha and all those who brought the sick and possessed to Jesus. The healing of a loved one or a friend is bound to have an impact on their supporter's own wellbeing and can be seen as a secondary healing. Hearing the voice of these anonymous characters is not difficult. But what of the crowd, the scribes and Pharisees, the Herodians and the disciples? Surely there are further examples of secondary and perhaps tertiary effects of the miraculous healings, aren't there? In addition, are there any parallels with the healing ministry today, and do the miracles have further effect even from their great distance in time to the present?

APPENDIX ONE

The Healing Miracles

	Mark	Matthew	Luke	John
The Synagogue Demoniac	1:21-28		4:33-38	
Peter's Mother-in-law	1:29-31	8:14-15	4:38-39	
Cleaning the Leper	1:40-45	8:1-4	5:12-16	
The Paralytic	2:1-12	9:2-8	5:17-26	
Withered Hand	3:1-6	12:9-14	6:6-11	
Gerasene Demoniac	5:1-20	8:28-34	8:26-39	
Jairus' Daughter part 1	5:21-24	9:18-19	8:40-42	
Jairus' Daughter part 2	5:35-43	9:23-26	8:49-56	
Woman Haemorrhaging	5:25-34	9:20-22	8:43-48	
Syro-Phoenician Girl	7:24-30	5:21-28		
Deaf Mute	7:31-37			
Blind Man at Bethesda	8:22-26			
Possessed (Epileptic?) Boy	9:14-29	17:14-21	9:37-43	
Bartimaeus	10:46-52	20:29-34	18:35-43	
Blind Men		9:27-31		
Malchus' Ear	14:47-48	26:51-52	22:49-51	18:10-11
Centurion's Servant		8:5-13	7:1-10	
Royal Official's Son				4:46-54
Blind Mute		12:11-32	11:14-23	
Mute Demoniac		9:32-34		
Woman's Son at Nain			7:11-17	
Crippled Woman			13:10-17	
Man With Dropsy			14:1-6	
Ten Lepers			17:11-19	
Paralytic at Bethesda				5:2-47
Man Born Blind				9:1-41
Lazarus				11:1-44

APPENDIX TWO

Chronological Ordering [54]

Official's Son	John 4:46 – 54
Synagogue Demoniac	Mark 1:21 – 28 with parallel
Peter's Mother-in-Law	Mark 1:29 – 31 with parallels
Cleansing the leper	Mark 1:40 – 45 with parallels
The paralytic	Mark 2:1 – 12 with parallels
Paralytic at Bethesda	John 5:2 – 20
Withered hand	Mark 3:1 – 6 with parallels
Centurion's Son (servant)	Matthew 8:5 – 13 with parallel
Widow's son at Nain	Luke 7:11 – 17
Gerasene demoniac(s)	Mark 5:1 – 20 with parallels
Jairus' daughter part 1	Mark 5:21 – 24 with parallels
Woman haemorrhaging	Mark 5:25 – 34 with parallels
Jairus' daughter part 2	Mark 5:35 – 43 with parallels
Two blind men	Matthew 9:27 – 31
Mute demoniac	Matthew 9:32 – 34
Syro-Phoenician girl	Mark 7:24 – 30 with parallel
Deaf mute	Mark 7:31 – 37
Possessed (Epileptic?) boy	Mark 9:14 – 29 with parallels
Man born blind	John 9:1 – 41
Blind mute	Matthew 12:22 – 24 with parallel
Blind man at Bethesda	Mark 8:22 – 26
Crippled woman	Luke 13:10 – 17
Man with dropsy	Luke 14:1 – 6
Lazarus	John 11:1 – 44
Ten lepers	Luke 17:11 – 19
Bartimaeus	Mark 10:46 – 52 with parallels
Malchus' ear	Mark 14:47 – 48 with parallels

---

[54] As suggested by Frank DeCenso, Jr. *Healings and Miracles of Jesus in Chronological Order.* Self published 1982

Bibliography

Bauckham, Richard. *Jesus and the Eyewitnesses: The Gospels as Eyewitness Testimony.* Grand Rapids, Michigan: William B. Eerdmans Publishing Company 2006

Braaten, Carl E. & Jenson Robert W. (Ed). *Sin, Death and the Devil.* Grand Rapids, Michigan: William B Eerdmans Publishing Co., 2000.

Brown, Les. (Ed). *Multiple Streams of Determination.* Dallas, USA: Wimbrey Training Systems, 2011

Browning, W.R.F. *Reader-Response Criticism: A Dictionary of the Bible.* 1997. Retrieved April 19, 2010 from Encyclopedia.com: *www.encyclopedia.com/doc/1094-ReaderResponseCriticism.html*

Bennett, George. *The Heart of Healing.* London: Arthur James Limited., 1971

Camery-Hoggatt, Jerry. *Reading the Good Book Well: A guide to Biblical Interpretation.* Nashville, Tennessee, USA: Abingdon Press, 2007.

Dale, David. *In His Hands: Towards a Theology of Healing.* London:Darton, Longman and Todd Ltd., 1989.

DeCenso, Frank Jnr. *Healings and Miracles of Jesus in Chronological Order.* USA: CreateSpace, 2007

Detweiler, Robert (Ed). *Semeia 31: Reader Response Approaches to Biblical and Secular Texts.* Atlanta, Georgia, USA: Sociaety of Biblical Literature, 1985.

Eagleton, Terry. *Literary Theory: An Introduction.* Oxford, GB: Blackwell Publishing, 1983.

Eve, Eric. *The Healer from Nazareth: Jesus' miracles in historical context.* London: SPCK, 2009.

Fish, Stanley. *Is There A Text In This Class: The Authority of Interpretive Communities.* London, Harvard University Press, 1980.

Fowler, Robert M. *Let the Reader Understand: Reader-Response Criticism and the Gospel of Mark.* Harrisburg, Pennsylvania, USA: Trinity Press International, 1996.

_____ *Who is "The Reader" in Reader Response Criticism?* Semeia 31 accessed 4 January 2010

Gooder, Paula. *Searching for Meaning: An Introduction to Interpreting the New Testament.* London: SPCK, 2008.

Green, Laurie. *Urban Ministry and the Kingdom of God.* London: SPCK, 2003.

Grundmann, Christoffer H. *He Sent then out to Heal: Reflections on the Healing Ministry of the Church.* Currents in Theology and Mission 33 No 5, 2006 pp372 - 378 Accessed 4 January 2010.

Harrington, Daniel. *Why do we suffer?: a scriptural approach to the human condition.* Franklin, Winconsin USA: Sheed & Ward, 2000.

Harrisville, Roy A. *A Critique of Current Biblical Criticism.* Word & World 15/2 (1995) pp206 - 213 accessed 4 January 2010

Heline, Corinne. *The Healing Miracles of Christ Jesus.* California, USA: New Age Press Inc., 1951.

Hinkle, Mary E. *People Like Us: Minor Characters in Matthew's Passion.* Word & World Volume 25, Number 1 Winter 2005. Accessed 4 January 2010

Hudson, Henry L. *At The Rumor of His Coming: Looking to Jesus for Miracles and Healing.* New York, USA: Universe, Inc, 2006.

Iser, Wolfgang. *The Act of Reading: A Theory of Aesthetic Response.* pp. 7, 30, 275, 728. © 1978 The Johns Hopkins University Press. Reprinted with permission of The Johns Hopkins University Press.

_____ *The Implied Reader: Patterns of Communication in Prose Fiction from Bunyan to Beckett.* London: The John Hopkins Press Ltd., 1974.

John, Jeffrey. *The Meaning in the Miracles.* Norwich: Canterbury Press, 2001.

Just, Felix. *Miracle Stories in the New Testament.* Article accessed 4 January 2010 http://catholic-resources.org/Bible/Miracles.htm

Kermode, Frank. *The Genesis of Secrecy: On the Interpretation of Narrative.* London: Harvard University Press, 1979.

MacLeod, George. *The Place of Healing in the Ministry of The Church.* Pamphlet published by Iona Community Pamphlets, date unknown

MacNutt, Father Francis. *Healing.* New York, USA: Bantam Books, 1974.

Masters, Peter. *Not like any other book: Interpreting the Bible.* London: The Wakeman Trust, 2004.

_____ *The Healing Epidemic.* London: The Wakeman Trust, 1988.

Polanski, Sandra Hack. *Identifying the Unnamed Disciples: An Exercise in Reader-Response Criticism.* Perspectives in Religious Studies 26 (1999), 193-202 Accessed 4 January 2010.

Resseguie, James L. *Narrative Criticism of the New Testament: An Introduction.* Grand Rapids, Michigan, USA: Baker Academic, 2005.

_____ *Reader-Response Criticism and the Synoptic Gospels.* Journal of the American Academy of Religion LII/2 accessed 4 January 2010.

Stuhlmacher, Peter. *Historical Criticism and Theological Interpretation of Scripture: Toward a Hermeneutics of Consent.* Eugene, Oregan, USA: Wipf and Stock Publishers, 1977.

Thiselton, Anthony C. *Hermeneutics: An Introduction.* Grand Rapids, Michigan: William B Eerdmans Publishing Co., 2009.

Tompkins, Jane P. *Reader-Response Criticism: From Formalism to Post-Structuralism.* London: The John Hopkins Press Ltd., 1980.

Twelftree, Graham H. *Jesus the Miracle Worker: A Historical and Theological Study.* Downers Grove, Illinois: IVP, 1999.

Willmington, Harold. *What You Need to Know About Jesus' Miracles: Healing.* Liberty University 2008. Article posted at DigitalCommons@Liberty University. Accessed 4 Jan 2010. http://digitalcommons.liberty.edu/will¬_know/32

Wimber, John. *Power Healing.* London: Hodder & Stoughton, 1986.

Wright, Stephen. *Reading Gospel Stories in the World Today.* Cambridge: Grove Books (B56), 2010.

Commentaries used:

New Bible Commentary. Leicester, England: Inter-Varsity Press, First printed 1953

The New Jerome Biblical Commentary. London: Geoffrey Chapman, First printed 1968

Carson, D. A. *The Pillar New Testament Commentary: The Gospel According to John.* Grand Rapids, Michigan: William B Eerdmans Publishing Co., 1991.

Edwards, James R. *The Pillar New Testament Commentary: Mark* Leicester: Apollos 2002

Farrell Morley, Marjorie. *A Journey Through St. Mark's Gospel.* Formby, England: Print Origination (NW) Ltd., 1993

France, R.T. *Tyndale New Testament Commentaries: Matthew.* Leicester, England: Inter-Varsity Press, First printed 1985.

_____ *Matthew: Evangelist and Teacher.* Exeter: Paternoster Press 1989

France, Dick. *The People's Bible Commentary: Matthew.* Oxford: The Bible Reading Fellowship, 1996.

Hauerwas, Stanley. *SCM Theological Commentary on the Bible: Matthew* London: SCM Press Ltd., 2006.

Hooker, Morna D. *Black's New Testament Commentaries: The Gospel According to St Mark.* London: A & C Black, 1991.

Horsley, Richard A. *Hearing the Whole Story: The Politics of Plot in Mark's Gospel.* Louisville, Kentucky: Westminster John Knox Press, 2001.

Kostenberger, Andreas J. *Zondervan Illustrated Bible Background Commentary: John.* Grand Rapids, Michigan: Zondervan, 2002.

Lindars, Barnabas. *New Testament Guides: John.* Sheffield, England: Sheffield Academic Press, 1990.

Lincoln, Andrew T. *Black's New Testament Commentary: John.* London: Continuum 2005

Moloney, Francis J. *Sacra Pagina* (series edited by Daniel J. Harrington S.J.): *The Gospel of John.* Collegeville, Minnesota.

Morris, Leon. *Tyndale New Testament commentaries: Luke* Leicester: Inter-Varsity Press, 1988.

Nickle, Keith F. *Preaching the Gospel of Luke: Proclaiming God's Royal Rule.* Louisville, Kentucky: Westminster John Knox Press, 2000.

Proctor, John. *The People's Bible Commentary: Matthew.* Oxford: The Bible Reading Fellowship, 2001.

Riches, John. *New Testament Guides: Matthew.* Sheffield, England: Sheffield Academic Press, 1996.

Telford, W. R. *New Testament Guides: Mark.* Sheffield, England: Sheffield Academic Press, 1995.

Tuckett, Christopher M. *New Testament Guides: Luke.* Sheffield, England: Sheffield Academic Press, 1996.

Contact the Author

To contact the author, please write to:

peteisfulofun@btinternet.com

Also From the Publisher

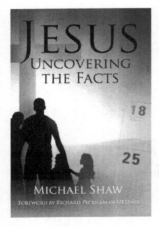

Jesus: Uncovering the Facts
Michael Shaw

The implications of Jesus' message and ministry are profound and challenging for every culture and generation. Therefore it is not surprising that the details recorded in the Bible accounts have been scrutinized for accuracy and sometimes criticized.

Can we rely on the accounts of Jesus' life, as described by Matthew, Mark, Luke and John? Does historical evidence give weight to the claims of the scriptures?

Michael Shaw tackles these difficult questions in this well-researched investigation into the life of Jesus, with particular emphasis on chronology. Filled with historical data, yet fast-paced and gripping, this book looks into some of the mysteries surrounding a world-changing historical figure and uncovers facts that have implications for our lives today.